Sociology
as an
Art Form

Sociology
as an
Art Form

Robert Nisbet

With a new introduction by *Paul Gottfried*

Transaction Publishers
New Brunswick (U.S.A.) and London (U.K.)

Library of Congress Catalog Number: 00-064814
ISBN: 0-7658-0756-4
Printed in the United States of America

Library of Congress Cataloging-in-Publication Data

Nisbet, Robert A.
    Sociology as an art form / Robert Nisbet ; with a new introd. by Paul Gottfried.
        p.cm.
    Originally published: New York : Oxford University Press, 1976.
    Includes index.
    ISBN: 0-7658-0756-4 (pbk. : alk. paper)
        1. Sociology—History—19th century. 2. Intellectual life. 3. Art and society. 4. Sociology—Philosophy. I. Title.

HM445 .N53 2000
301'.09—dc21

00-064814

In loving memory of S.N.

Acknowledgments

I have avoided, in keeping with the essay character of this book, footnotes and page references, contenting myself with simple identification of author and work in the text. There are, however, certain works which I have found extraordinarily valuable in the writing of my own book, and it is a pleasure to cite them here: Herbert Read, *The Art of Sculpture, Icon and Idea,* and *Art and Society;* Etienne Gilson, *Painting and Reality;* E. H. Gombrich, *Art and Illusion;* S. Giedion, *The Beginnings of Art;* Raymond Williams, *Culture and Society* and also *The Country and the City;* Jacques Barzun, *The Use and Abuse of Art;* and, not to be missed by anyone interested in the common nature of the artistic and scientific imagination, the special issue of the *Bulletin of the Atomic Scientists,* February 1959, with its often brilliant contributions by scientists and artists alike. Excepting only for the last-mentioned, none of the works just listed had come into my ken when the essential idea of this book was conceived (and published in an article in *The Pacific Sociological Review,* Fall 1962), but without the help provided by their explorations of the nature of art and its relation to the human mind, I should not have been able to expand that original idea into the present book. I gladly record here my obligation to all of these works. It is a pleasure also to express thanks once again to Stephanie Golden of Oxford University Press for her careful editing of this book and for her valuable suggestions regarding content and style.

Contents

Introduction to the
Transaction Edition

Although not considered one of his monumental works, unlike *The Quest for Community* (1953) and *The Sociological Tradition* (1967), *Sociology as an Art Form* (1976) was one of Robert Nisbet's favorites among his oeuvre. In conversations, he mentioned this text fondly and lamented the fact that it had not received the same attention as his more widely known studies of the fifties and sixties. This slim and carefully composed tract is one that unmistakably recalls the qualities of its author. Both the display of verbal facility and the predilection for nineteenth-century social theory were characteristic of Nisbet's texts. Equally so is the argument that runs through the work, that what marks the best of classical sociology is its relation to art and belles-lettres.

In an age when sociologists sought to imitate the quantifying methods and opaque idiom of the hard sciences, Robert Nisbet went against the current. He did so, moreover, successfully, becoming Albert Schweitzer professor in the humanities of Columbia University, the NEH Jefferson Day lecturer, and a widely read and translated social theorist. Nisbet was fond of telling his own highly personal account of growing up in America. The narrative would move from his working-class youth in Los Angeles (where he was born in 1913), through his years of teaching (1953–1972) in "the desert," as he referred to the University of California at Riverside, to his final professional

recognition at Columbia in 1974. Nisbet's popularity as an expositor
of sociology had much to do with this odyssey. A key reason for the
attractiveness of his work as a social theorist and for his numerous
publishing achievements has always seemed to be his capacity for
non-prescribed judgements. A self-described social conservative,
Nisbet spoke sympathetically about the organic, rural communities
of the medieval past and wrote blisteringly about the modern administrative state, from *The Quest for Community* to *The Present Age*
(1988). But Nisbet became and remained a religious skeptic, albeit
one with respect for the hierarchical principles of the Catholic Church
and for those of European counterrevolutionaries; and he disliked
intensely what he perceived as the vulgarly democratic character of
the religious right. One may suspect this contemptuous attitude,
though not always expressed, was extended to egalitarian religions
in general, e.g., to the Southern Baptists who professed Nisbet's own
social morality. In any case, readers who begin his books with the
belief that they will find there an authorial facsimile of Carry Nation
are invariably surprised. Like Spanish-American man of letters George
Santayana, Nisbet was a pious skeptic, who valued ritual and doctrine without believing in the transcendent sources of either. But he
was also as passionately concerned about public morals as any fiery
temperance preacher of the late nineteenth century.

His tastes in all things were unabashedly aristocratic. His tall,
handsome person was meticulously dressed, whatever the occasion,
and he and his equally prepossessing wife, Caroline, had a special
fondness for dainty-looking spaniels. But his notion of those who
are "best" was broad enough to embrace those he found exception-
ally studious, like his Asian and Jewish students to whom he ascribed
a particularly strong aptitude for his teachings. It is predictable that
in *Sociology as an Art Form* Nisbet would have kind words for thinkers who saw the world quite differently from him. In the same work he
praises unstintingly Joseph de Maistre, Karl Marx, Thomas Carlyle,
Max Weber, Frederic LePlay, Emile Durkheim, Edmund Burke, and
Ferdinand Toennies. While Nisbet certainly held settled views about
what constitutes good social theory, he found those views exemplified by revolutionary socialists as well as by critics of the French
Revolution.

By the same token, there is no confusing of the intellectual water-
shed that Nisbet treats as basic for his discipline. In *The Sociological*

Tradition, he attaches enormous theoretical importance to the critical investigation made by counterrevolutionaries of the French Revolution and of those social breaks it engendered. The radical practitioners of sociology, according to Nisbet, more often than not came along once the conservative ones had broken methodological and thematic ground. While these provocative successors, typified by Marx and Durkheim, labored in the service of progressive causes, they were also building upon the social analysis developed by unabashed reactionaries. Moreover, though Nisbet admired some luminaries of the Enlightenment, particularly the Baron de Montesquieu and David Hume, who anticipated his combination of religious skepticism and interest in social stability, in *Sociology as an Art Form,* sociological breakthroughs are traced primarily to counterrevolutionary Europe. Note the portrayal of German sociologist Ferdinand Toennies, "a member of liberal movements [who] voiced strong opposition to the currents of nationalism and anti-Semitism." Toennies, it is then explained, was "rather conservative in temperament, fundamentally antagonistic to a great many of the elements of economic modernity" and "something of a religious believer."

While Nisbet admittedly understates Toennies's commitment as a man of the Left, who supported Germany's Socialist Party and wrote a flattering biography of Thomas Hobbes as a radically materialist thinker, his more general point is well taken. Even the self-declared anti-conservative Toennies carried on the intellectual heritage of European conservatives; and in the detailed distinctions he made between *Gemeinschaft* and *Gesellschaft*, together with the defining characteristics he assigned to both, drew upon the images created by principled opponents of revolution. Such consequences, Nisbet would have argued, were inevitable as well as generally unintended, given the foundational role played by traditionalist defenders of *Gemeinschaft* in the "sociological tradition." These consequences were also unavoidable, in view of the recurrence of certain images, as an artistic and imaginative resource, in the same tradition.

There are paradoxes in Nisbet's thinking that readers would do well to make a mental note of. Both individualism and nationalism were, for him, related developments tied to the rise of the "centralized, territorial state." In *The Quest for Community*, the political entity in question is designated as "the single most decisive influence on Western social organization." (In my view, Nisbet, if anything, understates his case: He is defining nothing less than the most powerful, long-term influence ever exercised upon social organization. Hobbes's characterization of this administrative mechanism during its infancy as a "mortal deity" was prophetic as well as prescriptive.) Nisbet looked at the central state as a promoter of social disintegration in the course of advancing its power. States have advanced historically and habitually at the expense of "intermediate institutions," such as the family as a politically independent form of association, and have engaged in coordinated crusades, on behalf of the "nation" or "race" or aggrieved individuals and minorities. All such crusades proclaimed by centralized administration seemed, for Nisbet, similar in kind, strategically related power grabs undertaken to weaken by politicizing society.

Nisbet spoke quite positively of Albert Jay Nock, the individualist author of *Our Enemy the State* (1935) and *Memoirs of a Superfluous Man* (1943). As a soldier in the South Pacific during World War Two, he read Nock's brief against modern collectivism, an act performed almost simultaneously by Nisbet's later friend and fellow-conservative Russell Kirk, then stationed in the Great Salt Desert. But neither Nisbet nor Kirk shared the neo-Jeffersonian, libertarian vision that animated Nock's work. What brought them to it was fascination with its Tory Bohemian author, who abandoned his staid life as an Episcopal priest and paterfamilias to run off to New York and write elegant defenses of liberty as a social gadfly. And despite his occasional appeal to Jefferson as a Democrat, Nock more often held up the Virginian aristocrat who took all learning for his province and would have felt ill at ease in a mid-twentieth-century welfare state.

Though devotees of Nock, both Kirk and Nisbet fought long wars against American libertarians—and were roundly attacked by their adversaries as "statists." Though both of them may be charged with having been excessively nostalgic for vanished societies, Nisbet and Kirk were correct in their sociological and historical observations. A well-founded suspicion of the central welfare state does not disprove the Aristotelian axiom that man is a social being, as opposed to a self-inventing constructor of contracts. Nisbet believed that panicking critics of modern centralized government had embraced a theory of human behavior that was contradicted by our experience of social reality. Most important, Nisbet argued, the State actually increases its power by getting us to accept the "myth of individualism." As the official defender of individuals against oppressive social relations, modern administration has happily invaded, and continues to occupy, social spaces. Those who hope to understand what is taking place here, Nisbet insisted, should read Aristotle, Maistre, Tocqueville, and Burke, to find out how social atomization accompanies political tyranny. Nisbet also thought that libertarians, by misrepresenting human nature, made it harder to grasp why bureaucratic collectivism had taken over at the present time. People welcomed far-reaching political controls because they were born and disposed to live in communities as a condition for human fulfillment. By denying what was an easily observed truth, libertarians derailed the attempt to explain the threats to freedom that they claimed to be concerned with.

In the end, Nisbet was moved by personal loyalties as much as he was by any abstract principles. This, in my opinion, helps explain one of his most puzzling books, recently reissued by Transaction Publishers, *History of the Idea of Progress*. As a cultural pessimist, Nisbet had trouble talking to those who were high on the present age, which he emphatically disliked aside from its medical and technical benefits. But there was also the question of his pedagogic lineage. The scholar at Berkeley who sparked Nisbet's passion for social theory, Frederick Teggart, had lectured for decades on historical progress as a distinctively Western, Judeo-Christian idea. Nisbet's interpretive work is not identical to Teggart's treatment, but it does contain a lucid restatement of what his teacher had thought about the subject of progress. Nisbet writes as a worthy and reverential student, but as one who entertained reservations about the pivotal Western belief that he chose as his theme. He also was a fan of Winston Churchill, who in his eyes was a Tory battler against tyranny, but despised FDR, who had built the American welfare state and seemed unduly friendly to Soviet Russia. One of Nisbet's last books, an expanded essay on the "failed courtship" between FDR and Stalin, is an attempt to justify these sentiments. Here a farsighted Churchill is shown warning FDR, frantically but unavailingly, against the evidence of Soviet duplicity made manifest during the War. When I observed to my mentor, whose health was then failing, that Churchill had (in some cases even more recklessly) made the same mistakes as FDR, he admitted that alas this was true. He regretted having taken on this writing, while not being up to the task, and carrying it out without his customary thoroughness. "Perhaps I should never have published it!" he noted ruefully over the phone. I begged to disagree: Everything Bob Nisbet wrote, including this book, would continue to be studied. Though not an entirely dispassionate judgment, it will, I know, stand the test of time.

Sociology as an Art Form

Introduction

It occurred to me a number of years ago while I was engaged in exploration of some of the sources of modern sociology that none of the great themes which have provided continuing challenge and also theoretical foundation for sociologists during the last century was ever reached through anything resembling what we are today fond of identifying as "scientific method." I mean the kind of method, replete with appeals to statistical analysis, problem design, hypothesis, verification, replication, and theory construction, that we find described in our textbooks and courses on methodology.

The themes I refer to are well known to all in the social sciences and related areas: *community, masses, power, development, progress, conflict, egalitarianism, anomie, alienation,* and *disorganization.* There are others, but these will serve for the moment. Of the importance of these themes there can be no question. Without their presence, and above all their evocative power on the minds of sociologists for the last hundred years and more, sociology would be a drastically different body of thought indeed.

What also occurred to me in my explorations was the close affinity these themes in sociology had throughout the nineteenth century with almost identical themes in the world of art—painting, literature, even music—and, far from least, the close affinity of the sources of motivation, inspiration, and realization of these themes. Sociology and art are closely linked. We need only turn to the histories of literature, esthetics, and the arts generally to find ourselves in the presence of themes and aspirations which bear striking resemblance to those I have just identified in sociology. The relation of the individual to village, town, and city; the relation between city and countryside, the impact of authority, or dislocation of authority, upon human life; the pursuit of the sacred, the torments of anonymity and alienation: all of these are to be seen as vividly in the novels, dramas, poems, and paintings, even the musical compositions, of the ages as they are in the works of the sociologists from Tocqueville and Marx on.

Such reflections led me to this book which, from one point of view at least, can be thought of as a kind of prophylaxis against, not science, but *scientism*, which is science with the spirit of discovery and creation left out. I became increasingly conscious of the fact that not only is there no conflict between science and art, but that in their psychological roots they are almost identical. The unity of art and science exists most luminously in the motivations, drives, rhythms, and itches which lie behind creativeness in any realm, artistic or scientific.

Further reading led me to the realization that what had taken shape in my own mind regarding the essential unity of art and science had long before taken shape in other minds—scientific and artistic alike. Twenty-five hundred years ago Plato declared the unity of art and science, likening the work of the astronomer to that of the painter. We must, Plato wrote in *The Republic*, "use the blazonry of the heavens as patterns to aid in the study of those realities just as one would do who chanced upon diagrams drawn with special care and elaboration by Daedalus or some other craftsman or painter." When Kepler wrote, "The roads by which men arrive at their insights into celestial matters seem to me almost as worthy of wonder as those matters themselves," it would never have occurred to him that there was any significant difference between what he, the theologian, the philosopher, and the artist were engaged in. Marston Morse, distinguished contemporary mathe-matician, wrote a few years ago:

The first essential bond between mathematics and the arts is found in the fact that discovery in mathematics is not a matter of logic. It is rather the result of mysterious powers which no one understands, and in which the unconscious recognition of beauty must play an important part. Out of an infinity of designs a mathematician chooses one pattern for beauty's sake, and pulls it down to the earth, no one knows how. Afterwards the logic of words and of forms sets the pattern right. Only then can someone tell someone else.

Mathematics may not be the perfect exemplar of the sciences, which, after all, deal with the empirical and the concrete, as mathe-matics in its essence does not. But that is not the heart of the mat-ter. What is vital is the underlying act of discovery or illumination or invention that is the clue to all genuine creative work. The greater scientists have long been aware of the basic unity of the cre-ative act as found in the arts and in the sciences. A large and grow-ing literature attests to the awareness. Only in the social sciences, and particularly, I regret to say, in sociology, the field in which the largest number of textbooks on "methodology" exists, has aware-ness of the real nature of discovery tended to lag. Countless works in the social sciences reveal the inability of their authors to bear in mind the crucial difference between what may properly be called the *logic of discovery* and the *logic of demonstration*. The second is properly subject to rules and prescriptions; the first isn't. Of all sins against the Muse, however, the greatest is the assertion, or strong implication, in textbooks on methodology and theory con-struction that the first (and utterly vital) logic can somehow be summoned by obeying the rules of the second. Only intellectual drouth and barrenness can result from that misconception.

While reflecting on the unity of the creative act, I was struck fur-ther by what the *histories* of art and science have in common. It is well known to all historians of literature, painting, sculpture, archi-tecture, and the other arts that their subjects fall, or at least are commonly perceived to fall, into successive, sometimes recurrent, "styles." To the expert in painting, there is rarely any difficulty in distinguishing medieval from Renaissance, or, for the historian of architecture, Romanesque from Gothic. No greater difficulty attaches in the history of poetry so far as distinguishing between Elizabethan and Romantic—though no one would argue complete infallibility or the total separateness of styles from one another. The point is simply that for at least two centuries the histories of the arts have been written largely in terms of successive styles which are not unlike stages of development in evolutionary treatment of society.

Now science also reveals itself to us in terms of styles. This may be more difficult to demonstrate, and indeed of less value, in the physical sciences, but so far as the social sciences are concerned, and with them the social and moral philosophy from which they are descended, it is impossible not to be struck by the changes of style in a given social science over the period of a century or more. The style of sociology in the mid-nineteenth century is quite different from what later came into being in the age of Durkheim and Weber, and the informed observer will see a succession of styles— often really no more than fashions—in the sociology of our own century.

Finally, although the really vital unity of science and art lies in the ways of *understanding* reality, we should not overlook the important similarity of *means of representing* reality in the arts and sciences. We are all familiar, of course, with the portrait as it is found in painting, sculpture, and also literature. Portraiture is an ancient and universally recognized form in the arts. So is landscape, which we see so widely in painting, but also in literature and music. A landscape is the creative artist's means of representing some part of earth, sea, and sky as this has been distilled through the artist's own distinctive consciousness. Finally, the problem of motion, action, or movement has long been recognized by artists and by philosophers of art: the problem of using materials, whether in painting, sculpture, music, or literature, in such a way as to convey the dynamic sense of flow, of movement through time and space.

All of this, as I say, is well known in the arts. But what is not well known, as I came to realize, is that sociology in its history has faced precisely the same problems, and has utilized, *mutatis mutandis*, precisely the same means or forms for conveying an understanding or sense of reality to others. Thus, as I show, a great deal of what is most important in sociology consists of, in effect, landscapes of the social, economic, and political setting in nineteenth- and early twentieth-century Western Europe. What Tocqueville and Marx, and then Toennies, Weber, Durkheim, and Simmel, give us in their greatest works, ranging from *Democracy in America* and *Capital* to Toennies on *Gemeinschaft* and *Gesellschaft* or Simmel on *Metropolis*, is a series of landscapes, each as distinctive and compelling as any to be found among the greater novels or paintings of their age. The fascination with the contrast between countryside and city that we observe among the Impressionists is rivaled among the major sociologists, equally interested in the effects of the rural and the urban upon human life.

The same holds with portraits. What artist of the period gave us role-types in his novel or painting more evocative than what we draw from Marx about the bourgeois and the worker, from Weber about the bureaucrat, or from Michels on the party politician? Role-type, as I have indicated, is the sociologist's compromise between the generality or recurrence of human experience and its individuality. But so is it the artist's compromise.

How alike too are the sociologist's and the artist's efforts to endow subject matter with what Herbert Read, the art historian and critic, has called "the illusion of motion." No mean esthetic skill is involved in Marx's depiction of capitalism as a structure in motion, in Tocqueville's rendering of equality as a dynamic process, or Weber's of rationalization.

Scientists Marx, Weber, Durkheim, and Simmel were without question. But they were also artists, and had they not been artists, had they contented themselves with demonstrating solely what had been arrived at through aseptic problem design, through meticulous verification, and through constructions of theory which would pass muster in a graduate course in methodology of sociology today, the entire world of thought would be much poorer.

One additional point: I have also been struck repeatedly by the number of instances in which visions, insights, and principles native to sociology in its classical period were anticipated, were set forth in almost identical shape and intensity, by artists, chiefly Romantic, in the nineteenth century. We cannot take away from Tocqueville, Marx, Weber, and the other sociologists the visions for which they are famous: visions of mass society, industrialism, bureaucracy, and the like. But we live in ignorance if we do not see clearly these same visions, albeit stated differently, in the earlier writings of such minds as Burke, Blake, Carlyle, Balzac, and a score of others whose reactions to the democratic and industrial revolutions created a pattern of consciousness that the sociologists, and others in philosophy and the sciences, fell into later. Over and over, it seems to me, we are made aware in the history of thought of the primacy of the artist. I mean this in a double sense. Not only is the artist likely to precede the scientist in recognition of the new or vital in history—with a Blake castigating the machine-driven factory long before anything but complacent acceptance had occurred to a social philosopher or scientist—but, in one and the same person, it is the art-element of consciousness that is likely to generate, through intuition and other states best known to art, the elements we are prone to describe as scientific.

I have no doubt there will be sociologists to declare that their field is diminished or distorted by likening it to art, whether in source of imagination or in the forms through which imagination is communicated. But, then, there will surely be artists who, should they read these pages, will have much the same reactions. For a long time now, though only really since the early nineteenth century, we have perpetuated the delusion that art and science are by their nature very different from one another. It is high time this delusion is ended, and reluctant sociologists may take heart from the fact that for a good while the really great scientists of our century, in physics, mathematics, biology, and other spheres, have been emphasizing the basic unity of art and science.

I

The Sources of Imagination

Sociology is, without question, one of the sciences, but it is also one of the arts—nourished, as I argue in this book, by precisely the same kinds of creative imagination which are to be found in such areas as music, painting, poetry, the novel, and drama. Nor is sociology in any sense alone in this kinship with the arts. Behind the creative act in any science, physical or social, lies a form and intensity of imagination, a utilization of intuition and what Sir Herbert Read has called "iconic imagination," that is not different in nature from what we have learned of the creative process in the arts.

It would be wrong to declare that art and science are the same. They are not. Each has its distinctive, identifying marks, chiefly those of technique and mode of demonstration. It is not wrong, however, to stress the fact that in the history of Western thought down until the nineteenth century, there was little if any consciousness of art and science as separate areas of inspiration and work. Not in the medieval age, nor in the Renaissance, the Age of Reason, or the Enlightenment was any substantial differentiation made between, say, the operations of a Michaelangelo and those of a Kepler.

We do, however, make such a differentiation today, and the principal argument of this book is that the differentiation tends to hide more than it reveals. What is common to art and science is vastly more important than what is different. I cannot help thinking that the renewal or reinvigoration of idea and theory we so badly need in sociology in the present age, indeed in all the social sciences, would be greatly accelerated if sufficient awareness of the unity of art and science, especially with respect to the sources of imagination in each area, were present at all levels of teaching and research.

The first misconception that must be overcome is this: that whereas the function of science and scholarship is to search for the truth, the illumination of reality, the function of art, in any of its manifestations, is simply to express the beautiful or to provide us with vicarious experience as the substitute for understanding of truth. But what Herbert Read has written in *Art and Society* is very much to the point here:

The essential nature of art will be found neither in the production of objects to satisfy practical needs, nor in the expression of religious or philosophic ideas, but in its capacity to create a synthetic and self-consistent world . . . a mode, therefore, of envisaging the individual's perception of some aspect of universal truth. In all its essential activities, art is trying to tell us something; something about the universe, something about nature, about man, or about the artist himself.

The artist's interest in form or style is the scientist's interest in structure or type. But artist and scientist alike are primarily concerned with the illumination of reality, with, in sum, the exploration of the unknown and, far from least, the interpretation of physical and human worlds.

And just as the artist must be seen as concerned directly with the realm of knowledge, so must the scientist be seen in the light of what we call esthetics. We have the testimony of a good many scientists on this point. The discernment of beauty in a given hypothesis, the recognition of esthetic achievement in a proposition or formula, the appreciation of elegance in the setting forth of a result—all this, as is by now well known, occupies a large place in science. Strange as it may seem at first thought to the outsider, the fact is well established that many a theory or principle has been chosen by its scientist-author because of its esthetic properties.

Nor is there conflict between the esthetic and the practical or utilitarian. Most of man's most fundamental inventions, Cyril Stanley Smith of MIT tells us, made their initial appearance in the context of the artistic, the esthetic, rather than in that of strict necessity. "Innovation and discovery," Professor Smith writes, "require esthetically-motivated curiosity; they do not arise under the pressure of need, although of course once new properties of matter or new mechanisms become known they are available for use." Metallurgy itself, Smith writes, "began with the making of necklace beads and ornaments in hammered, naturally-occurring copper long before 'useful' knives and weapons were made."

Wherever initial impetus may arise, though, the close relation between art on the one hand and science and craftsmanship on the other is very old and deep. The elitist image possessed since the nineteenth century by the artist makes us forget the position he held in the social order for a great many centuries. In the Middle Ages and down through the Renaissance, the painter and sculptor were regarded like any of dozens of other craftsmen. Art as we know it today was regarded indeed as one of the servile occupations in many places. Etienne Gilson in *Painting and Reality* cites Vasari to the effect that Michaelangelo himself had great difficulty as a boy in finding time for the work he loved, such was the antipathy of his father and other elders in the family to his "wasting" his time on matters considered base in the illustrious household in which Michaelangelo grew up. "The fact that painting is manual work," Gilson writes, "has visibly influenced the course of its history."

But how analogous this is to the history of science! Think only of the centuries in which those who sought to experiment with nature were obliged for respectability's sake to conduct their work virtually in secrecy; such was the lack of esteem in which manual work was held. Not until the nineteenth century could science be deemed suitable for college or university.

In so many respects, then, art and science are alike. The greater scientists, among whom I include the greater sociologists, with Max Weber perhaps foremost in this respect, have been and are aware of this cognateness, as indicated by Weber's profound insistence upon the primacy of what he called *Verstehen*, of an understanding that penetrated to the realm of feeling, motivation, and spirit. Any artist who has ever examined what underlies his own creative work would agree with Weber on the crucial importance of understanding that is at once rooted in intuition, in "iconic imagination," and in what is drawn from experience and observation.

There is in science and art alike the drive on the part of the creator to get away from the ordinary world of perception and of what we like to think of as common sense. Einstein once wrote: "I agree with Schopenhauer that one of the most powerful motives that attracts people to science and art is the longing to escape everyday life." It is not that either art or science is an ivory tower, a refuge or retreat. Each is, on the contrary, a means of bringing to highest level a form of observation and an intensity of understanding that is so often thwarted by what Robert Bridges once called the "endless literalness" of what lies around us. A theorem in mathematics, a principle in physics, a symphony, a sonnet, a novel, each is "escape" if we like, but it is in no sense an escape from reality or truth; only from the conventionalities and literalnesses which press upon us and within which we are obliged to spend so great a part of our individual lives. I find it instructive that the word "theory" comes from the same Greek root as the word "theatre." A tragedy or comedy is, after all, no less an inquiry into reality, no less a distillation of perceptions and experiences, than a hypothesis or theory that undertakes to account for the variable incidence of murder or marriage. When Shakespeare declared: "All the world's a stage, /And all the men and women merely players./They have their exits and their entrances,/And one man in his time plays many parts . . .," he had reached a level of understanding that has only in very recent years become explicit in the writings of a few sociologists.

It is a mistake to think of creativeness as some special power with which only geniuses are endowed. What Livingston Lowes in his study of Coleridge, *Road to Xanadu*, wrote is pertinent:

"Creation," like "creative," is one of those hypnotic words which are prone to cast a spell upon the understanding and dissolve our thinking into haze. . . . [W]e live, every one of us—the mutest and most inglorious with the rest—at the center of a world of images. . . . Intensified and sublimated and controlled though they be, the ways of the creative faculty are the universal ways of that streaming yet consciously directed something which we know (or think we know) as life. Creative genius, in plainer terms, works through processes which are common to our kind, but these processes are superlatively enhanced.

The crucial word in Lowes's passage is of course "images." We cannot do without them, in science or in art. What else is imagination but the moving around in the mind, restlessly, compulsively, so often randomly, of *images* with which to express and to contain some aspect of perceived reality? Herbert Read, in *Icon and Idea*, writing of "the constructive image," quotes the twentieth-century artist Gabo:

"With indefatigable perseverance man is constructing his life, giving a concrete and neatly shaped image to that which is supposed to be unknown and which he alone, through his constructions, does constantly let be known. He creates the images of his world, he corrects them, and he changes them in the course of years, of centuries. To that end he utilizes great plants, intricate laboratories, given to him with life; the laboratory of his senses, and the laboratory of his mind; and through them he inverts, construes, and constructs ways and means *in the form of images* for his orientation in this world of his."

It was Bacon and Descartes—two of the most imaginative and creative minds in all of Western thought—who did, alas, the most to establish the idea that truth is the straight-line result, in Bacon's rendering, of sensory observation attended by a method of induction that yields laws or principles, and in Descartes's terms, of a rigorous process of deductive reasoning from the self-evident. Each thought that by concentrating upon a *method*, truth, the discovery of knowledge, could be made available to all human beings equally. That no major scientist ever has proceeded in his work along either Baconian or Cartesian lines, any more than has any major artist, has not prevented the consecration of method by these two genuinely powerful minds from exacting a dismal toll, especially in the social sciences. For what neither Bacon nor Descartes realized—or if either realized it, he remained mute—is that apart from "icon and idea," apart from the seminal image, indeed a plethora of images, all the dogged adherence to method imaginable is destined to futility and barrenness. Michaelangelo began with an image in creating his *Pietà*, but so did Faraday in developing his dynamo and electromagnetic induction, and so did Einstein in developing his theory of relativity.

"The evolution of the human mind is a single process," wrote the late Eugene Rabinowitch, eminent physical scientist,

revealed with different intensity, different clarity, and different timing—in its various manifestations—in art, science, philosophy, social and political thought. It is like a fugue, or an oratorio, in which different instruments or voices enter in turn. . . . The voice of the artist is often the first to respond. The artist is the most sensitive individual in society. His feeling for change, his apprehension of new things to come, is likely to be more acute than that of the slower-moving, rational, scientific thinker. It is in the artistic production of a period, rather than in its thinking, that one should search for shadows cast in advance by coming events, for prophetic anticipation.

Repeatedly the intellectual-cultural history of the West has shown these words to be true. I can recall vividly when the priority of art was first thrust upon my own mind. It was in the course of my first visit and fascinated wandering through the halls of the great Uffizi art museum in Florence. In that museum, where each room represents, so to speak, an age or part of an age in the West since the late Middle Ages, it was possible to see not only the changing images of man and society in the sculptures and paintings, but also the precedence these had in time over the identical changes in image which are to be found in the history of philosophy and science. In art, long before philosophy, the fateful transition from the communal-spiritual envisagement of man to the envisagement we have been accustomed to in the West ever since the Renaissance is vividly to be seen. It is art that forms the real bridge between medieval communalism, rooted so deeply in the lives of people in their towns and families and guilds and neighborhoods, and the increasingly mechanical, power-driven, ego-dominated, and sensate society we have seen spread throughout Western society from the Renaissance on, and in our own century over the rest of the world.

I shall have more to say about the implications to sociology and its larger themes of this momentous historical change. For the moment, though, it is the priority of art, of the artist's imagination in all discovery or interpretation, that I wish to stress. In terms of initial intellectual experience, what the artist and scientist have in common is their desire to comprehend the external world, to reduce its apparent complexity, even chaos, to some kind of ordered representation. In a very real sense the first art in mankind's history is also the first science. The famous pictographs left in the caves of Dordogne by Cro-Magnon man in the Late Paleolithic are not to be thought of as simple acts of decoration. They are ventures in the transfer of the unknown to the known.

"Artistic activity begins when man finds himself face to face with the visible world as with something immensely enigmatical. . . . In the creation of a work of art, man engages in a struggle with nature not for his physical but for his mental existence." The words are those of Conrad Fiedler, German philosopher of art in the nineteenth century, quoted by Herbert Read in his important book *Icon and Idea*, a book appropriately subtitled "The Function of Art in the Development of Human Consciousness." Read tells us, with a wealth of illustration, "that art has been and still is the essential instrument in the development of human consciousness."

So it is. And it is also the essential instrument of the scientific, not least the sociological, consciousness. The itch of curiosity we correctly find at the core of genuine science had its earliest human expressions in art. Without exception, the first renderings or representations of space, mass, motion, of the relation of flora and fauna to environment, and of the nature of man and of culture and society are first found in art: in pictograph, painting, sculpture, ballad, epic, and lyric.

There is never anything tidy, organized, or systematic in genuine discovery. "The discoveries of science," wrote the late Jacob Bronowski, Nobel laureate, in *Science and Human Values*, "the works of art, are explorations—more like explosions of a hidden likeness. The discoverer or artist presents in them two aspects of nature and fuses them into one. This is the act of creation, in which an original thought is born, and it is the same act in original science and original art."

Those words could well be engraved over the entrance of every building devoted to the physical and social sciences, particularly the latter. How different things would be, one cannot help reflecting, if the social sciences at the time of their systematic formation in the nineteenth century had taken the arts in the same degree they took the physical sciences as models. What happened in so many instances is that the form, the rhetoric, and the manner of science was taken over by those engaged in the study of human beings but not the real heart, the psychological heart, of physical science at its very best. Again I come back to the difference between the logic of discovery and the logic of demonstration. It was the latter, in all its nineteenth-century certitude, determinism, and mechanism, that seems to have had the greatest impact upon those who, like Comte and Mill, were seeking the absolute, final, and irrefutable science of man. The really distinguished and seminal minds of the century in the social sciences, however, clearly recognized the affinity between the sources of science and art. None of these minds was ever caught in the crippling fetters placed by curriculum upon so many youthful minds at the present time.

This is not to say that the minds I speak of were not disciplined, were not constrained, even coerced, by the values inhering in any body of thought or practice. It is only to say that none of them was ever required to jacket himself in the restrictive types of intellectual bureaucratization which are the staple of so many of the textbooks in methodology and theory construction lying around us at the present time.

We need only think of the crimes committed in the name of "proof" or "verification" or "validation" in the classroom today.

That one must, in science at least, seek the kind of truth that is available, at least theoretically, to others goes without saying. It does not, however, follow that research or investigation is valueless if it cannot be subjected to objective verification by others at every step of the way. An able historian, David L. Hull, has shown us how thoroughly acceptance of Darwin's theory by the scientific community in the mid-nineteenth century was retarded by the widespread belief that theories such as his must be "proved" and that, inasmuch as Darwin had admittedly not provided proof in the form demanded, the theory was therefore valueless. As we know, it was not, in fact, until—through quite independent channels—the resources of Mendelian genetics were brought to bear that "proof" of any kind whatever of Darwinian natural selection became possible. Suppose Darwin had been checked by "theory constructionists"!

Sir Peter Medawar has properly emphasized the dangers of the naively ritualistic uses of "proof" and "verification":

People tend to use the word "proof" in the empirical sciences as if it had the same weight and connotation as it has in logic and mathematics, for we do indeed in the strictest sense of the word *prove* Euclid's theorems to be true by showing that they follow deductively from his axioms and postulates. But with the empirical sciences and especially with ideas of the generality of evolution, gravitation, and even the roundness of the earth, it is not so much a question of finding "proofs" as of expounding the grounds for having confidence in them.

The great harm of the present consecration of method, including theory construction, is that it persuades students that a small idea abundantly verified is worth more than a large idea still insusceptible to textbook techniques of verification. Many years ago Florian Znaniecki wrote of the damage done to questing young minds by methodology's preeminent place in the sociological curriculum:

This influence consists in substituting tabular techniques for intellectual methods, and thus eliminating theoretical thinking from the process of scientific research. . . . A condition can be foreseen—indeed it has been reached—when anybody who has learned by heart the various technical rules and formulae of statistics, with no other education whatsoever and no more intelligence than a moron, will be able to draw from a given material all the conclusions which statistical problematization makes possible. . . . The role of creative thinking in science, according to this conception, will be reduced to the function of formulating hypotheses which are to be tested by technical means. But we have seen that the only hypotheses statisticians ever have formulated, and ever can formulate, in view of the unavoidable limitations of their method, are no more than superficial generalizations of common-sense practical reflection. There is little place for creative thought and even less for scientific progress in this kind of problematization.

Of course science is concerned with problems, with questions rooted in empirical observation as well as reflection. The greatest advances of sociology, as with any science, have come indeed when some obsessing problem was being dealt with by a mind of genius. So is the artist interested, however, in problems which are presented by reality, by the world of experience and fact. Without perception of problems there would be, as John Dewey correctly noted many years ago, no real thought at all; only musing, reverie, simple association, daydreams, and the like. It is the challenge of some problematic aspect of experience that precipitates all of us into such thinking as we ever do, and we often find ourselves surprised by how well we have dealt with some sudden, difficult problem.

But from the incontestable truth that science begins with perception of problems, it does not follow that scientific discovery is wholly or even largely the simple consequence of what is today called, in courses and treatises on method, "problem-defining" and "problem-solving" thought. Too often what are called problems are actually more like the puzzles which amuse us and which do indeed call forth powers of ingenuity. The science-historian Thomas Kuhn has correctly stressed that a great deal of science, what Kuhn calls "conventional science," is made up of answers to what are at bottom only puzzles. One might, by adaptation of terminology, say pretty much the same of conventional art. It too is in its way the solution of a "puzzle" presented by experience or visual reality. Only rarely, in science or in art, are the kinds of problems dealt with which are more than the perplexities, conundrums, and puzzles presented ordinarily in life and which we meet through one or other of the means suggested by conventional science or art.

Despite the candor of many distinguished scientists and artists in telling of their work, and despite what we have been able to learn in more general terms about creativity, there is still a great deal that we do not know about it. But this much is clear. The problems, insights, ideas, and forms which come to the artist and to the scientist seem to come as often from the unconscious as the conscious mind, from wide, eclectic, and unorganized reading, observing, or experiencing, from musing, browsing, and dreaming, from buried experiences, as from anything immediately and consciously in view. They come, as Arthur Koestler has shown us in several of his extraordinary works, as often from the "left-handed" processes of feeling and intuition as from the "right-handed" channels of logic, empirical directness, and reason. It is one of the most brilliant living physical scientists, Willard Libby, who has declared *essential* scientific method to be "rape followed by seduction."

If this is true, are we not then obliged to draw the conclusion that anything resulting in the shrinking of the field of experience and imagination, in the stunting of the intuitive process, in the routinizing or ritualizing of the creative faculties, is to be regarded with all the hostility we give, as scientists, philosophers, and artists, to limitations of any kind, political or other, to freedom of thought?

I do not see how we can do other than describe as limitations to freedom of thought certain of the reigning Idols of the Mind or, as I prefer to say, Idols of the Profession, in contemporary sociology. The Idols Francis Bacon found and identified in the schools of thought and universities of his day continue to exist in our time, and nowhere more obviously than in the courses and textbooks and treatises which seek to represent sociology as a composite—a very *ordered* composite, it must be emphasized—of precise rules for designing problems, arranging data, achieving hypotheses, verifying results, and, in triumphant fulfillment, setting forth what is called theory. How many book reviews in the professional journals, after extolling a given work for its intrinsic interest, then conclude with what are intended as devastating words to the effect that this work "does not advance our theory" or worse, "is unlikely to affect sociological theory"? To which, all we can say is: *What theory?*

For of all the Idols of the Mind or Profession regnant today the worst is that which Bacon might have placed among his Idols of the Theatre: the belief, first, that there really is something properly called theory in sociology, and second, that the aim of all sociological research should be that of adding to or advancing theory. At its worst this idolatry takes the form of veneration for the grand system. It is evidence of the credulity of sociologists that, despite the lamentable fate of the grand systems of the nineteenth century—those of Comte, Spencer, and Ward among others—the mere mention of the words *theory* and *system*, and even more to the point, *grand* or *systematic theory*, arouses reactions of an almost religious kind. It is a truth we should never tire of repeating that no genuinely good or seminal work in the history of sociology was written or conceived as a means of advancing theory—grand or small. Each has been written in response to a single, compelling intellectual problem or challenge provided by the immediate intellectual environment. William James did not err in labeling as "tender minded" all systems-builders, whether religious or lay, and placing under "tough minded" those who welcome and deal with life in its actual concreteness.

It is a byword that art abhors all systems. So does the creative process generally. We have the poet Blake's aphorisms, set down in *Jerusalem:* "Art and Science cannot exist but in minutely organized Particulars." And "To Generalize is to be an Idiot. To Particularize is Alone Distinction of Merit. General Knowledges are those Knowledges that Idiots possess." In recent years we have learned what dismal results in the arts come from the artist's seeking to bend poem, novel, or brush to the needs of some abstract esthetic theory acquired from philosophers, critics, or ideologues. We are less likely to observe precisely the same results, from analogous causes, in sociology, but they are present.

I have been referring to "theory" in the by-now accustomed sense of didactic bodies of interrelated principles and corollaries, abstract, general, encompassing, and, if possible, geometrical in character, through which the concreteness of ordinary experience and observation is supposed to be illuminated. Interspersed among such principles and corollaries are invariably to be found generalizations drawn, quotation-fashion, from the light and leading of the profession. Such theory, as we find it today in sociology, is much more like a primitive version of what used to be called metaphysics. I can find nothing evocative in it; quite the contrary, it is a barrier to the evocative and creative.

If, however, by "theory" we have in mind only the illumination, the sense of discovery, that accompanies any genuinely fresh study of a piece of the world we live in, then there can be no harm in its use. After all, in this modest sense, we draw "theory" from such works—not one of them consciously directed to or stimulated by theory in the grand sense—as Simmel's *Secret Society*, Sumner's *Folkways*, the Lynds' *Middletown*, Riesman's *The Lonely Crowd*, Goffman's *Asylums*, Homans' *English Villagers*, Merton's *Science, Technology and Society in Seventeenth-Century England*, or, for that matter, any of literally dozens of major works in history—hardly a field in which grand theory is often sought. In such works the universal is found, as it should be, in the concrete!

Quite as fatal to creative thought as the passion for systems is the current consecration of what, for want of a better phrase, is known as "theory construction." This is at bottom no more than old-fashioned methodology in the social sciences dressed up in pretentious and faddish clothing. The same crippling error to be found in manuals on method is found, though far more grandiloquently registered, in books on theory construction. This error is, as I have several times stressed, the belief that techniques peculiar to mere *demonstration* of something can be utilized also in the *discovery* of something. Deeply rooted in all such works is the delusion that the creative imagination works logically, or should work logically, with everything neat and tidy. It is no wonder that the computer has become the veritable symbol, as well as the worshipped master, of so much so-called social science in our time. In the computer everything can be programmed so neatly, with results brought forth in such well-ordered fashion, that it is no wonder questions, issues, and problems have become so mechanical and conventionalized in contemporary sociology.

But neither a textbook on theory construction nor the computer will ever substitute for what is at the heart of true science and true art: the individual's own creative faculties. The computer will no more endow the scientist's mind with creative inspiration, or even actual result, than the brush or pencil will the artist's. It is hard to think of anything more fatal to discovery or invention than the idea that the creative act can be generated by properly following the rules of logic.

"The creative scientist," writes Marston Morse, "lives in 'the wildness of logic' where reason is the handmaiden and not the master. I shun all monuments that are coldly legible. I prefer the world where the images turn their faces in every direction, like the masks of Picasso."

Reality is the quest of the artist as of the scientist, and failure to keep this in mind is bound to result in the production of the meretricious or the merely pretty in art, or in science the trivial and the banal. If the greatest themes of science in human history have also been the themes of art, the reason is not far to seek: the common quest to understand reality. And in this quest it is art that is historically and also, us I have argued here, logically prior. "The very possibility of science," Etienne Gilson tells us in *Painting and Reality*, "presupposes the existence of realities produced by art, or by a still higher power than that of artists and of art. . . . If there are forces, powers, or energies in the world which are productive of novelty, the only discipline that can directly communicate with them is art, any art, provided only it keeps faith with its own essence, which is that of a creative activity in the order of formal being. . . . Art introduces us to a world of forms whose final completion is the outcome of a sort of biological growth."

But so does science introduce us to a world of forms, each of which is the outcome of creative processes analogous to organic coming-into-being. The materials of any science, the data, as we commonly refer to them, are certainly not to be disregarded. The ultimate objective of any science is that of explaining these materials or data as we encounter them in experience and observation. But the act of explaining entails the employment of forms, configurations, and patterns which are at bottom the scientist's means of expressing the connections and interrelationships he finds in his universe of data. And in his use of forms, so defined, the scientist is obliged to be aware of the past, that is, what has been done before him. In the words of the physicist John Rader Platt, "In science . . . the past closes doors for us. The latecomers must nibble on auxiliary theorems and minor consequences. After Schrödinger's paper appears, no physicist wants to solve the hydrogen atom by that method again, except as a pastiche."

It is not different in art. The great painter, novelist, or poet can by the heroic size of his achievement close the gates in his special area to all who follow. As T. S. Eliot writes: "Milton made a great epic impossible for succeeding generations; Shakespeare made a great poetic drama impossible; such a situation is inevitable and it persists until the language has so altered that there is no danger, because no possibility, of imitation. . . . For a long time after an epic poet like Milton, or a dramatic poet like Shakespeare, nothing can be done."

Precisely the same holds, though we do not always phrase it so, in science. The individual scientist is competing, as it were, with the dead just as with the living. So, obviously, is the artist. The wells of creativity lie in time as well as space; neither science nor art can divorce itself from what has been done in the past, for in one way or another the past stays with us constantly. It forces us, though artists and scientists alike, to be constantly on the search for new opportunities of expression. Malraux has written: "Every artist of genius . . . becomes a transformer of the meaning of the world, which he masters by reducing it to forms he has selected or invented, just as the philosopher reduces it to concepts and the physicist to laws."

It is in this light that we can join John Rader Platt in foreseeing a time when "these historically separate disciplines will cease to be separate, when the various transformations of the meaning of the. world will come to form a continuous spectrum, and it will not be possible to say of a great creator: 'He is an artist' or 'He is a physicist,' any more than it was possible of Leonardo."

It is sometimes said, in effect: yes, one may assent to the unity of art and science when one is referring simply to the psychological sources of each, to the primal act of intuition or prescience that, so to speak, puts one on the scent of the unknown. But science, in contrast to art, is experimental ultimately, whereas art is not. But this will not hold up at all. Artists constantly experiment; each picture, or effort at one, each trial at a musical composition or a paragraph in a story or novel is at bottom an experiment. And in art as in science, experiments tend to follow conventionalized routines, except where the ground-breaking genius is at work. Among sociologists it was Max Weber, in *Science as Vocation*, who called attention to the relation of art and experiment in science.

The experiment is a means of reliably controlling experience. Without it, present-day empirical science would be impossible. There were experiments earlier; for instance, in India physiological experiments were made in the service of ascetic yoga technique; in Hellenic antiquity, mathematic experiments were made for purposes of war technology; and in the Middle Ages, for purposes of mining. But to raise the experiment to a principle of research was the achievement of the Renaissance. They were the great innovators in *art*, who were the pioneers of experiment. Leonardo and his like and, above all, the sixtenth-century experimenters in music with the experimental pianos were characteristic. From these circles the experiment entered science, especially through Galileo, and it entered theory through Bacon. . . .

The last point I will make on the affinity of art and science, of art and sociology, has to do with the vital contexts of each. I suggest they are very much alike; that the most fertile conditions of science, on the historical record, are identical with the most fertile conditions of art. Historical periods great in art are often great in science and in technology. In these contexts the free will of the artist or scientist is vital, allowing only for the fact that all will or inspiration works within circumstances which are historically evolved. There are certain common rhythms in art and science, and these demand freedom on the part of the artist and scientist to obey these rhythms, to follow the itch of curiosity wherever it leads, and to be unconstrained by the commands of government or other large-scale organization. Great art and great science have commonly emerged in small, informal groups where a few like-minded individuals can stimulate one another in autonomous intimacy. Repeatedly in the history of thought we find that where the great individual, the titan, exists, there exist with him, often unsung and unheralded, a tiny few others almost as great. These may be teachers, colleagues, or pupils, or a mixture of the roles, but the small, intimate, autonomous association is a commonplace in the history of both art and science.

In our day, both individual and small-group creativeness has become more and more difficult to sustain, especially in the scientific world. We have seen large-scale, bureaucratized science come into being since World War II, bolstered up by the mammoth government or foundation grant, and, along with this, we have seen government increasingly taking over the vital determination of the ends and objectives of science. Thus government "declares war" on cancer, on environmental pollution, on poverty, or, as it were, on the moon—leading to a gigantic, monopolizing concentration of resources in some single direction. Only rarely do such government-decreed "wars" come even close to succeeding. Much commoner is actual interference with the processes of knowledge. If, as is more and more frequently asserted—even and especially by scientists themselves—we seem to be running beyond our actual intellectual resources at the present time, in the physical and social sciences alike, to be confronted more and more frequently by the manifest failure of knowledge, with the Muse in frequent danger of being dethroned, the reason lies in swollen expectations on the one hand and loss of vital creative contexts on the other. The creative impulse, whether in art or science, simply cannot be commanded, as one commands minds and bodies in a military or bureaucratic enterprise. Success with such projects as the atom bomb and the moon-landing—each the result, in fact, *not* of any crash program buttressed by billions of suddenly produced dollars but, rather, of long years and decades of patient, unheralded work by individual scientists responding to their own needs and desires without the slightest conception of either atom bomb or moon-landing off in the future—has, alas, created the dangerous illusion that governmental command accompanied by endless supplies of money can elicit just about anything from scientists. But, in all truth, it is as fatuous to suppose that a great scientific achievement can be legislated or decreed into being, with great money and vast organizations appropriated, as it would be to suppose that a great novel, symphony, or painting could be so created. Science and art have, basically, their own vital, creative contexts, and we interfere with these at our own peril. The essential barrenness of the creative impulse in the arts when, as in time of war in the democracies and in the totalitarian states constantly, artists are made, in effect, to wear uniforms, has for long been recognized. Precisely the same barrenness exists in the theoretical sciences in such circumstances, as we are coming only more slowly to realize. And the reason for this lies in the essential unity of the arts and sciences, whether conceived as actual achievements or in the light of their motivating psychological and social conditions.

2

Themes and Styles

"Variations on a theme by . . ." The reader may fill in the name Bach, Haydn, or Mozart as he likes, or that of any number of composers, for as everyone knows a great deal of the history of music consists of conscious, explicit "variations" performed by one composer upon the works of others (sometimes, it should be added, such variations less than explicit and acknowledged!). So, as we have learned, do poets do variations on works of predecessors, and so also do painters, though it is probable that in neither poetry nor painting is the practice as well recognized and honored as in music.

It is not different, really, in philosophy and in the physical and social sciences, though this fact is not generally recognized, at least in this particular light. Themes are crucial to the philosophical and scientific disciplines; just as crucial as to the arts. In philosophy "variations on a theme by Plato" could serve as the title of literally thousands of works. In more modern times political science came into existence quite literally as a series of sixteenth- and seventeenth-century variations on major themes set down by Machiavelli, Bodin, and Hobbes. And for contemporary sociology "variations on a theme by Weber or Durkheim" would describe a great deal of published writing. The same is true in the physical sciences. Gerald Holton has shown the importance, from Kepler to Einstein, of certain basic themes in science.

Some of the themes which Professor Holton has identified in physical science are found also in the arts, and, of greatest import here, in sociology and the other social sciences. He writes:

The (usually unacknowledged) presuppositions pervading the work of scientists have long included such thematic preconceptions as these: simplicity, order, and symmetry; the primacy of experience *versus* that of symbolic formalism; reductionism *versus* holism; discontinuity *versus* the continuum; hierarchical structure *versus* unity; the animate *versus* the inanimate; the use of mechanisms *versus* teleological or anthropomorphic modes of approach.

Above all, Holton tells us, the "thematic dyad of Constancy and Change" has been a powerful one in Western science, ever since Parmenides and Heraclitus.

Clearly, these are as much the concern of the artist as they are of the scientist. As themes they may be tacit, unacknowledged, even unperceived in any direct sense, but they are not the less directive. With very little adaptation of terminology, it would be possible to organize a history of architecture or painting or sculpture around these same themes, or most of them. And, as I say, they are certainly vividly evident in the history of social philosophy and the social sciences.

It should be observed that the artist's concept of "styles" is also appropriate to our understanding of this history of philosophy and science. I refer here not so much to the "style" of the individual artist or scientist but rather to those patterns or configurations of intellectual and artistic activity which we are able to see successively manifesting themselves in the history of a given discipline. Every art historian or critic if he is knowledgeable has the capacity for recognizing in the work of an individual artist, even if he is anonymous, the style, which may be translated commonly into "age" or "period" within which that individual artist did his work. I do not say absolute certainty is ever possible in this process of detection, for idiosyncracies and eccentricities, or deliberate distortions, can occasionally disguise. But it is exceedingly rare all the same for any individual piece of work in art to escape the dominant marks of the style of the period when it was created.

The late Karl Mannheim, exemplary sociologist of knowledge, recognized the affinity of art and science in the concept of style. "It is indeed," he writes, "the history of art which provides us with a term capable of doing justice to the special nature of history of thought. . . . Everyone will accept the notion that art develops in 'styles,' and that these 'styles' originate at a certain time and in a certain place, and that as they grow their characteristic formal tendencies develop in a certain way." As we shall see there are and have been distinct *styles*, as well as themes, in sociology.

In *The Gothic Revival*, the art historian Kenneth Clark writes: "The idea of style as something organically connected with society, something which springs from a way of life, does not occur, as far as I know, in the eighteenth century." It does occur, however, as Clark points out, in the nineteenth century, and almost from the very beginning. In the literary writings of Madame de Stael, in the philosophical works of Maistre, Bonald, Coleridge, and Southey, as well as in the earliest sociological writings, those of Saint-Simon and Comte, there is the profound and obsessive sense of style as something going well beyond any individual artist, thinker, or craftsman, as being rooted in the social scene, in the social landscape, and thus helping to give identity to the individual. In 1800, in *Literature Considered in Its Relation to Social Institutions*, Madame de Stael wrote: "My purpose is to examine the influence of religion, custom, and law upon literature, and the influence of literature upon religion, custom and law." Throughout her remarkable work the author deals with the reciprocal relation between literature and society, seeing the former, its themes, styles, and configurations, as interwoven with those of the latter. All life, all art, all thought, become inseparable from the condition of *belonging:* to class, community, family, and church.

The first evidence of competence in any historian of painting, sculpture, or literature is his capacity for recognizing "styles" or, depending upon context, "ages," which usually mean pretty much the same thing. The style of the Middle Ages in the rendering of human beings and of landscape is clearly very different from the style of, say, the Quattrocento, just as this is very different from the style regnant in the eighteenth century. And within the larger style of a period or age of history there is the style that becomes associated with a Giotto or Michaelangelo or Leonardo, or with a Chaucer, Shakespeare, or Dryden. Grant all we will the individuality of art in its concrete manifestations, these, as even the most cursory inspection of museums or illustrations in textbook histories suggests, fall, with rare exceptions, into categories we label styles or periods.

It is not different in the history of philosophy or of science. In the former we refer to such "styles" as Scholasticism, empiricism, rationalism, associationism, idealism, pragmatism, and the like. In the history of science, as such masters as Duhem, Sarton, and Butterfield have shown, the works of scientists, whether experimental or theoretical or both, fall into distinguishable clusters through time which are nothing but styles. And, as Mannheim emphasizes, social science, most obviously, has its styles, which enable us to distinguish the work of a Ricardo from a Keynes, an Austin from a Maine, a Comte from a Weber. And what is true of styles is equally true of themes in art and in science.

A style or theme may or may not be the product of some one great piece of work. It is fair to say that in poetry Milton established a style, a pattern of themes, forms, and rhythms, that had almost immediate and then lasting effect. Aristotle's *Physics* had this effect in the ancient and medieval ages. Lyell's *Geology*, with its pervasive emphasis on uniformitarianism in the study not just of the earth but of all nature, without doubt created a style in science, one to which Darwin's *Origin of Species* plainly belongs, though this takes nothing away from the individuality of Darwin's work. Great works can often create what Thomas Kuhn calls "paradigms," which are, from my point of view, essentially styles—of approach, content, and result. Kuhn writes: "Men whose research is based on shared paradigms are committed to the same rules and standards for scientific practice. That commitment and the apparent consensus it produces are prerequisites for normal science, i.e., for the genesis and continuation of a particular research tradition."

There are, quite evidently, "paradigms," in Kuhn's sense, in the history of literature and all the arts. Here, as in science, such paradigms or styles are the consequence over and over of some great, dominating individual creator: an Aristotle or Milton. But it would be wrong, I believe, to assume that all styles may be traced back to some one seminal work by an identifiable individual. Ill-understood though contexts of inspiration are, we are obliged, on the historical evidence, to recognize them as such, and to be aware of their transcendence of any specific individual or group of individuals. It is no retreat to mysticism or to the supernatural to posit the existence in time of what have been variously called "the spirit of the age," the *Zeitgeist*, and, at low levels, "fashions and fads." Each of these is actually a style of thinking and working, to which a word such as "realism" or "naturalism" or "Romanticism" or "classicism" tends to be applied so often in the histories of art and literature. So are there styles of work in physics at the present time, and in biology, and, most certainly, in economics and sociology. Different styles may succeed one another, obviously, but they may also coexist.

At the center of any given style lies what can only be called a theme, or a cluster of themes. Theme carries with it a more active, positive, and dynamic character than does the word style. Implicit in any theme is at once a question being answered, more or less, and also an ordering of experience and observation in a special focus.

Our concern in this book will be with certain dominant themes in sociology, but before turning to them, or even identifying them, it will be useful to describe the concept of theme in a little detail. The first thing to be said is that many of the themes to be found in art and science have their origins in very ancient myth, ritual, metaphor, and other expressions of mankind's effort over countless millennia to convert chaos to order. Myth is probably man's oldest means of endowing life with meaning; certainly its origins are lost in obscurity. Suffice it to say that every people we know, when first it comes into historical view, is rich in possession of myths concerning such matters as origin, relation to gods and other peo-

ples, place in the cosmos, and historical sequences and events, that
we ordinarily think of as religion. For a very long time in human
history, myth—which as used here refers not to something necessarily false but rather to any large belief that serves at once to ratio-
nalize experience and to integrate opinion, attitude, and experience—contained all of the vital psychological elements which are
today found variously in religion, art, and science. As all historians
of Greek science and philosophy have stressed, the themes and
problems with which the pre- and post-Socratic philosophers oc-
cupied themselves sprang in the first instance from immemorial
myths.

Out of myth come art and drama, as is well known, but out of it
also come the beginnings of philosophic and scientific imagination.
The essential character of any myth, as such varied students as
Malinowski, Jung, and Eliade have emphasized, is its concern with
reality. Mircea Eliade writes for many students of the subject when
he tells us that myth "is always the recital of a creation; it tells how
something was accomplished, began to *be*. It is for this reason that
myth is bound up with ontology; it speaks only of *realities*, of what
really happened, of what was fully manifested."

Greek fascination with the phenomenon of change and growth
and development originated, as is a matter of clear record, with
mythical thinking, the kind we find in such a myth as that of
Demeter where, in dramatic and arresting form, the whole mystery
of the seed and plant is set forth. Of all the gods and goddesses,
Demeter was the most cherished by the Athenians, and we can easily understand how, even after the beginning of rational philosophy
and science in the sixth century B.C., worship of Demeter continued without let. Myth, in sum, underlay and also undergirded
Greek philosophy.

The same may be said of metaphor. Human thought in the large
is almost inconceivable apart from the use in some degree of metaphor. Whenever we identify one thing with another—one commonly better known in nature than the other—we are engaging in
metaphor. "The mind is a machine." "Societies are organisms." "A

mighty fortress is our God." All of these are instances of metaphoric construction. Metaphor is no simple grammatical device, a
mere figure of speech; not, that is, in its fullness. Metaphor is a
way of knowing—one of the oldest, most deeply embedded, even
indispensable ways known in the history of human consciousness.
"Metaphor," writes Herbert Read, "is the synthesis of several complex units into one commanding image; it is the expression of a
complex idea, not by analysis, nor by direct statement, but by sudden perception of an objective relation." The poet Wallace Stevens
writes of the "symbolic language of metamorphosis," thus telling us
correctly that in every metaphor a process of conceptual transformation takes place.

It is easy for the positivist to dismiss metaphor as "unscientific,"
as a substitute for rational or scientific reasoning, as belonging to
the enchanted areas of life—art, religion, and myth. But from metaphor proceed some of the dominating themes of Western science
and philosophy, as well as art. I shall mention three only, but they
will serve to suggest the vastness of the influence of metaphor.
They are *growth*, *genealogy*, and *mechanism*. Consider the first. Only
in the organic world of plants and animals is growth literally and
plainly to be seen: the development from seed, through ordered
and regular phases, of stages which are contained potentially in the
seed from the very beginning. Growth is change, yes, but when we
declare some change a manifestation of growth in the social sphere
we are speaking metaphorically. We are endowing an institution or
social structure with processes drawn from the organic world. Few
perspectives, few themes, have been more vital in Western thought
than that of growth or development, which is a conceptual product
of metaphor.

The same is true of genealogy. That organisms produce organisms which produce organisms *ad infinitum* is both obvious and
ancient as a proposition. However mysterious the conception process itself may have been to primitive man tens of thousands of
years ago, he was well aware, he had to be aware, of the phenomenon of birth and of the succession of generations linked in iron

necessity. If organisms produce organisms, thus leading to fixed genealogy, why cannot it be said that other, nonorganic things also
operate genealogically in time? Such as events, actions, and all the
other things which make up the human condition through the pass-
ing of time. Hence the genealogical character of the kinds of
thought, or conceptual construction, we call *history*, *chronicle*, or the
narrative. "First this and then . . ." The familiar words are the
very stuff of historical narrative, whether sacred as in the Old Tes-
tament, artistic as in the epic, or rationalist as in the latest work of
history coming forth on, say, the American nation. The notion of
the genealogical connectedness of things is by now a virtually ineradicable aspect of the human consciousness, quite possibly one of
the "structures" dealt with by Levi-Strauss, Noam Chomsky, and
others concerned with the nature of consciousness. But it is not the
less metaphoric in foundation.

Third is the mechanism or machine. From the time man devised
his simplest tool or engine, the model was in existence for a likening of other, complex or unknown areas of life to the basic operations of the mechanism. In every machine, however simple, there
are certain elements of motion held in equilibrial stability and, once
started, not requiring additional thought or attention, save possibly
replenishment of a source of energy. How easy then to liken society, man himself, the entire universe, to a machine. Thus the origins of what we call mechanism in philosophy.

Behind the themes of art and science, then, lie, in many cases,
myths and metaphors. But I do not limit themes, even the grandest
and oldest in human consciousness, to either myth or metaphor.
The sources of themes are multifold, to be found in ordinary experience, perception, and observation; but also in self-awareness and
introspective thought.

Several common aspects of all artistic and scientific themes are
worth emphasizing before we turn to those of sociology. I list them
in no particular order of importance.

First, a theme, in the sense here used, contains certain implicit
or explicit assumptions about reality or a part of reality, certain

"unconscious mental habits," to use Arthur O. Lovejoy's phrasing. Of themes we may say what Lovejoy says of "unit ideas" in the history of thought: they are often so much a matter of course, so widely taken for granted within a given field, that they are rarely if ever examined critically. I have mentioned the theme of growth. So deeply is this a part of the whole Western tradition in the study of human society that it almost never occurs to us to question whether social phenomena do indeed obey the same imperatives of change which are to be found in the organic world. In the Enlightenment, as Carl Becker has shown us in his fascinating *Heavenly City of the Eighteenth-Century Philosophers*, simplicity was in every sense of the word a theme. It was virtually taken for granted that reality in any sphere would be known by its simplicity. Thus when Adam Smith wrote his influential *Wealth of Nations*, he was setting forth in detail what he called "the simple system of natural liberty" that would prevail in the economic order if only surrounding impediments and barriers were expeditiously removed. For Smith, and also for the *philosophes* in France at the same time, complexity bespoke interruptions of the natural order in any area, economic, political, or social. Simplicity was, in sum, a theme of the Enlightenment in that it underlay nearly all the concrete efforts toward either understanding or reconstruction in social thought.

Second, a theme has many of the characteristics which are attributed by artists and scientists—and especially by those interested in language and thought—to *structures* in their descriptions of our relationships with the external world. What has come to be called structuralism in science and art is, at bottom, the assertion that knowledge of the external world enters the mind not in the form of the raw data which atomistic psychologists once declared to be the true beginnings of all thought, but rather in the form of patterns, *Gestalten*, configurations, or structures already formed. The idea of simple, direct relation of "mind" to "environment" is rejected in this view, and replaced by the idea of preexisting structures of thought, or, rather, of the thinking-process, which act as filters, so to speak, taking over the immensely complex work of

screening, assimilating, and organizing sensory data at the outset.
Few mistakes have been greater than that which has recurrently
reigned in philosophy making us see the mind as a blank tablet in
the beginning with simple, additive experience writing impressions, ideas, and conclusions on it. The capacity for any kind of
thought (thought, that is, sharply differentiated from mere reflex-
responses) is inseparable, as we have come to realize, from structures which from the beginning make of human thought the highly
selective thing that it is. The mind, as the biologist C. H. Wadd-
ington has written, "can neither mirror nor construct reality. Instead, for the mind, *reality is a set of structural transforms* of primary
data taken from the world." (Italics added.)

Precisely the same function is found in *themes:* those of the
worlds of science and art alike. When a given theme assumes historical importance in painting or poetry, in physics or chemistry,
in sociology or psychology, it acts in the cultural sphere precisely
as does a structure or "structural transform" in the sphere of individual cognition. "Reality" is indistinguishable from what is perceived under the influence of, in interaction with, theme. However
unique or distinct a single artist or scientist may seem, close study
reveals his relation to themes which transcend him in time and
place.

Themes give unity to individual diversity in each of the ages or
periods of history, either general history or specific. Thus, *reason*—
in contrast, say, to religious revelation—gave unity to the varied
quests and assertions in social and moral thought in the seventeenth
and eighteenth centuries. However variegated the individual
works, they were given a common character by the theme of reason
or rationalism as the acknowledged basis of, or path to, truth in
this era, thus making it possible to refer with considerable justice to
the Age of Reason. In music, a common theme, or rather set of
themes, identifies such a period as the Baroque, to the degree that
the general listener (and at times even the specialist) has difficulty
in recognizing the individual distinctiveness of one composer in the
period as compared with another. One thinks of the transcending

theme of Christianity, and within this large theme, the component themes of the Nativity, the Crucifixion, the Virgin, and others, in the art and architecture of the Middle Ages. The rise of the modern conception of the *individual*, free and secular, liberated, as it were, from religious community, is of course a hallmark of the painting of the Italian Renaissance. Individuality in its own right thus becomes a theme. From the eighteenth to the twentieth century, in both Europe and the United States, the emergence of the large city, *metropolis*, furnished an underlying theme for a host of novelists, ranging from Defoe in the eighteenth century to Dickens, Zola and many others in the nineteenth, and to such men as Dreiser, Herrick, Dos Passos, and Nelson Algren in the twentieth. In more recent times, roughly since the 1950s, the individual self, *consciousness*, reflexive awareness, have given a certain priority to subjectivism in literature and art. And no one acquainted with the history of sociology during the last decade or two will be unaware of the dominance of precisely these same styles and themes in this area. Once again the lesson is repeated: the theme of subjectivism so evident in the 1960s in sociology was well preceded in time by the identical theme in art and literature.

It is needless to multiply examples. It will suffice to say that a style or theme in any field, art or science, has a generality and also an evocative power sufficient to direct the motivations and energies of countless individuals each of whom may be unaware that what he is doing in laboratory, studio, or study takes on significance as part of a prevailing and also coercive style or theme.

What are the dominant themes of sociology? Let me first indicate what I regard as the sovereign themes of the social sciences, of social philosophy, in the West during the past two millennia. For there are, as a moment's reflection suffices to tell us, different and descending levels of generality of style, theme, and comparable pattern of intellectual interest. From the time of the ancient Greek philosophers, especially after Socrates came on the scene, down through Rome, the Western Middle Ages, the Renaissance, the Age of Reason, all the way to our own day, several deep, underly-

ing, persisting themes are to be seen amid the vast profusion of individual works on man and his place in the world.

First, without question, among these great themes is that of the
individual—his nature, mind, desires, and soul—conceived as a distinct, even separate entity. Not until there had taken place through
historical processes a certain separation of the individual from what
Durkheim calls the "primal social mass" was it possible for individual human beings to begin to reflect upon themselves as distinct,
real, even primary elements of consciousness. So far as the West is
concerned, the first great period of this kind of reflecting was about
midpoint in the first millennium B.C. Since then it is noteworthy
that all major periods of "individualism" in social thought have followed, or attended, the kind of social dislocation and uprooting of
tribe, village, and family we see first so vividly in Greece of the
sixth century B.C.

Second is the theme of *order*. It follows from the first. Only
when a profound sense of the separateness of individual from social
order had entered the speculative, philosophical mind, attended by
sharp perceptions of disorder, disintegration, and breakdown, was
it really possible for order itself to become a conscious, obsessing
problem. Not by mere accident or coincidence did Western social
philosophy arise in the first instance amid the conditions of breakdown, as these were so widely perceived, which followed the disas-
trous Peloponnesian wars, with a defeated Athens suddenly become the setting of the kinds of thinking which were represented at
their highest by first Plato, then Aristotle. The requirements of
order in society have been detailed since in a variety of ways—
religious, political, economic, military, and sociological—but
whether it is Plato writing *The Republic*, St. Augustine *The City of
God*, Hobbes his *Leviathan*, Adam Smith *The Wealth of Nations*, or
Auguste Comte his foundation work in sociology, *The Positive Philosophy*, the common problem, the shared, overriding theme of
each, is the achievement and undergirding of social order.

Third is the theme of *freedom*. This too is a deep preoccupation
that reaches us from the speculations of the Greeks, that is never

absent during intervening epochs of thought in the West, and that, however it may be defined, is as profoundly rooted in Western consciousness as is either individuality or order. Indeed the supreme objective of Western philosophy and science so far as the study of man is concerned is that of somehow reconciling the demands of individuality, order, and freedom.

Fourth and last among the great themes is *change*. No people in the ancient world was as obsessed by the phenomenon of change as the Greeks. From the time Heraclitus pronounced everything to be in process of flux, or growth, down to the writings of our own day, the nature of change—and also of development and progress—has fascinated Western man. Just as the reconciliation of order and freedom has been an abiding quest in Western thought, so has the reconciliation of order and change. To find the seeds of order in change and, conversely, the seeds of change in order, this has been and is one of the dominant objectives of Western social thought, a powerful theme in itself.

But if the four themes just described are the master themes of Western social thought since the ancient Greeks, it does not follow that there are not other, more specialized, more distinctive, themes to be found in each of the several branches of social thought, in each of the social sciences which came into formal existence in the nineteenth century. My concern here is with sociology, and it is useful to identify those themes which—resting, as it were, on the base provided by the master-themes described above—have guided the energies of sociologists since Comte brought the discipline of sociology into being, and which may be seen vividly in the writings of those such as Tocqueville, Marx, Le Play, Toennies, Weber, Simmel, and Durkheim among the Europeans and in the United States in the works of Sumner, Cooley, Ross, Mead, and Thomas.

A decade ago, in *The Sociological Tradition*, I described these themes in detail, pointing out how they may be seen as forming in their combination the essential structure on which have been built the diverse concepts and theories of modern sociology. These themes are: *community*, *authority*, *status*, the *sacred*, and *alienation*.

They came into existence in the setting created in Western Europe by the two great revolutions of modern times, the industrial and the democratic. To the minds of Comte, Tocqueville, and, later, Weber, Durkheim, and Simmel, the European social landscape was one of devastation, a condition caused by the shattering impact, as these minds perceived it, of revolutionary democracy and rampant industrialism upon such historic structures as kinship, local community, guild, church, and social class. Even Marx, optimistic though he may have been about the eventual outcome, was far from insensitive to the themes I have mentioned. They may be seen in one form or other in all of his earliest writings, *The Communist Manifesto* included. It was the perceived *absence* of legitimate community, authority, hierarchy, and sacred belief in nineteenth-century Western Europe that led the sociologists to these themes and also to the theme of alienation, for it was modern man's lack of roots in legitimate society that led ineluctably, the sociologists believed, to his sense of estrangement and isolation from both membership and moral value.

These selfsame themes are to be found in the literature and art of the nineteenth century, where they also provide a kind of structure within which works of great individual diversity are produced. The sense of social devastation, of uprooting of the individual, is no less penetrating, anguished indeed, in the writings of Coleridge, Southey, Carlyle, Chateaubriand, Balzac, Stendhal, Heine, Nietzsche, and Wagner as in those of the sociologists. And to find the basis of acceptable authority, community, and hierarchy, to recover the foundations of a spirituality that would do for modern man what Christianity had done for medieval man, all this was as much the preoccupation of the humanist in that century as it was of the sociologist.

Indeed, as the rest of the chapters of this book make manifest, humanist and sociologist worked in very large measure through common understandings, perceptions, and even forms. It is with no violation of context or content whatever that I have chosen to describe sociology in its great formative age, the age that reaches from Tocqueville and Marx through Weber, Durkheim, and Simmel, in the terms of "social landscape," "portrait," the "illusion of motion," and what I have called "the rust of progress." Precisely as painting or literature may be, and of course often has been, seen in the terms of landscape, portrait, and so on, so may sociology be seen thus. To set forth the cultural and social landscape of Western Europe, to identify distinctly the dominant role-types, to seek to derive dynamic strength, motion, or movement from structure and setting, and to assess the costs to community and individuality of modernity—all this is as much the objective of a Marx or Simmel as it is of a Blake, Coleridge Balzac, or Dickens among writers and of a Hogarth, David, Millet, or Daumier among those who made line, light, and shadow serve the cause of illuminating reality. And, whether in artist as such or in sociologist, the influence of the themes I have mentioned—*community, authority, status,* the *sacred,* and *alienation*—is unmistakable.

Without doubt the sociology of the age I am concerned with produced much else: ideas and concepts of role, structure, function, development, interaction, and so on. I do not question this. But precisely as historians of science and of art find these areas deeply textured by major themes which provide at once challenge and order to individual scientists and artists, so may we look beneath the layer of theory, idea, concept, and empirical study that first meets the eye in the study of sociology and find analogous themes.

3
Sociological Landscapes

The sociological writing of the nineteenth century is as rich in landscapes as any other sphere of the creative imagination. Taking the century as a whole and including literature, music, and painting, as well as the social sciences, in our purview, it would be hard to find any period in Western history more productive of landscapes.

The dictionary tells us that a landscape is "a portion of natural scenery, usually extensive, that may be seen from some special viewpoint." The last three words are crucial; there is no means of observing landscape save from one's special viewpoint. When we speak of *a* landscape in an art gallery, we have some piece of topography before us, but only as it has been transmuted, filtered through the artist's perceptions, consciousness, and style. Hence the striking differences found among paintings of a single scene not only by different artists but by the same artist at different moments of his career. "Just as a real landscape is spontaneously seen as a work of nature," writes Gilson in *Painting and Reality*, "so also is a painted landscape, or musical composition, seen or heard with full awareness of the fact that its origin lies in the creative power of the artist."

The social and cultural landscape is as much the province of the sociologist—or novelist or poet—as the physical setting is of the painter. Human behavior is single, not something that divides neatly into separated, insulated compartments labeled "political," "economic," "religious," and the like. In this respect human behavior is not different from the physical landscape, which is also a unity and not a congeries of compartments to which the terminology of the physical sciences can give separated existence. The same terrain will be "seen" by the geologist, the physicist, the chemist, the wildlife conserver, and the landscape designer in quite different ways corresponding to the quite different interests and stereotypes which lie in their minds.

Far from least among sociology's contributions in the nineteenth century is the distinctive ways in which its practitioners saw the landscape in human affairs that had been so largely created by the two great revolutions. The art element in sociology is just as evident in its landscapes as in its portraits and its efforts to deal with movement or change. Not quantitative, empirical science following any of the contrived prescriptions of current textbooks in methodology or theory construction, but the artist's vision, lies behind such concepts as mass society, *Gemeinschaft, Gesellschaft,* social status, authority, the sacred and the secular, alienation, anomie, and the other signal reactions to the European social landscape in the nineteenth century that we properly associate with the development of sociology. And here too, just as with respect to sociological portraits, there is much in common between sociology and each of the several forms of art prominent in the century. I shall come to the sociologist's portraits in the next chapter. Here we shall look at some of the diverse landscapes which were suggested by the European social scene to the major sociologists of the age. Without exception, these social landscapes are shared by sociologists and artists, and also without exception, each of these landscapes may be seen taking shape in the works of poets, novelists, and painters in the nineteenth century well before it becomes clearly visible in the writings of Marx, Toennies, Weber, Durkheim, and Simmel.

Let me begin with some valuable words written in our own century by the late W. H. Auden in *The Dyer's Hand:*

In grasping the character of a society, as in judging the character of an individual, no documents, statistics, "objective" measurements can ever compete with the single intuitive glance. Intuition may err, for though its judgment is, as Pascal said, only a question of good eyesight, it must be good, for the principles are subtle and numerous, and the omission of one principle leads to error; but documentation, which is useless unless it is complete, must err in a field where completeness is impossible.

In the sociological landscapes I have selected, the truth of Auden's words will be seen repeatedly.

THE MASSES

No rendering of the social landscape created by the two revolutions is commoner in the nineteenth century than that represented by the word *masses*. It has many synonyms: rabble, mob, crowd, hoi polloi, canaille, populace, people among them—all pointing to the large numbers of persons thrust suddenly, as it seemed, into prominence by the forces which had destroyed or weakened the fabric of the old, traditional, aristocratic order. In time the word would assume favorable significance among socialists and other radicals whose programs were built upon the perspective, however idealized, of the masses as opposed to small special-interest groups such as capitalists or aristocrats. But in the beginning the idea of the masses carried distinctly pejorative associations to those using it.

It is not the factor of size that gives meaning to the idea of the masses, though there were many besides Thomas Malthus to be made apprehensive by the sheer increase in population that was taking place. Rather, it is the *composition* of the population, as this composition was perceived by artists, philosophers, and sociologists from the time of the French Revolution on. Basically, this composition was predicated upon the notion that attending the revolutionary changes of the time was an atomization of the social order, a conversion of what had been immemorially a genuine social order marked by predominance of kinship, religion, class, and neighborhood into what now seemed nothing less than a horde of separated human particles.

It is important to stress the subjective quality inherent in this perception, this rendering (there is no other word for it) of the demographic landscape. For in fact not only were family, religious, and class ties still to be seen everywhere, even in those parts of the West where revolutionary forces were most clamant and the tides of industrialism strongest, but new types of association could be seen emerging: labor unions, mutual aid societies, cooperatives, and utopian communities among them. I think it would be difficult indeed to substantiate on any strictly quantitative and objective measurement the idea of the masses, as we so characteristically find the idea in the writing of the century. But the element of what the dictionary calls "special viewpoint" and what Gilson refers to as the "creative power of an artist" is, as I argue throughout this book, not to be ignored. Never mind that on purely empirical grounds it was no more possible to see "the masses" in the nineteenth century than in, say, the seventeenth; the fact remains that in the later century the idea assumed commanding importance, affecting not only the nature of what was perceived but also a whole pattern of other ideas which would almost certainly not have been present in European writing had there not been the underlying vision of a once-organic, articulated, and rooted society converted by political and economic change into a mass society.

The idea of the masses, in the artist's and sociologist's sense here used, probably begins with Edmund Burke's strictures on both the French Revolution and the rise in his day of the new economic class based not upon land but upon the much more liquid and mobile forms of wealth associated with money, credit, and shares of stock. One does not have to read deeply in Burke to find vivid evidences of his disdain for this economic class and his repugnance for the kinds of economic enterprise native to it: speculation, incessant buying and selling for quick gain, and the conversion of traditional relationships of hereditary status into those of mere contract. Even more striking is Burke's perception of the atomizing effects

upon a population of the kinds of "arbitrary" power he saw em-
ployed, with a justification rooted in rationalism and natural rights,
by the French revolutionaries upon their fellow countrymen.

From Burke the vision of the masses, of the disunited multitude,
the atomized population, passes quickly to conservatives and Romantics in the early part of the nineteenth century. Sometimes the
vision is set in humanitarian context, with sympathy for and pity
of the masses foremost in the writer's mind. We see this in the "industrial novels" of the century, in some of the poems of Shelley
and Southey, and in the philosophical writings of Coleridge, Carlyle, and Matthew Arnold. Other times the idea of the masses is set
forth in more pejorative terms, with contrast to aristocratic society
made central. But what we find in every context is the intuitive,
iconic, and often blinding sense of society undergoing processes of
leveling, atomization, and abstraction resulting in enlarging
numbers of people devoid of neighborhood, religion, social class,
kinship—above all, of *community*. It is the contrast, variously expressed, between community and mass society that looms above all
other contrasts in the social writing of the century. We cannot see
clearly or understand the sociological landscape of the masses
unless we look also at the renderings of community lost and community gained, or to be gained, in the literature of the time. Few
intellectual events in the century are more important than the rediscovery—through perceived absence in the surrounding scene—
of the importance of those communal ties which had been so detested by the *philosophes* in the preceding century.

Thus the fascination with such evidences of community as could
be found or imagined, a fascination seen in the works of
Wordsworth, Coleridge, Carlyle, and Matthew Arnold in England,
and in those of Chateaubriand, Tieck, Schiller, and Goethe on the
Continent. In a great deal of the Romantic writing of the early
nineteenth century there is to be seen a fascination with themes
provided by the individual in his relation to the soil, to village, to
family, and to other reminders of the traditional society that had
been so severely damaged, it was believed, by the impacts of indus-

trialism and mass democracy. The often-noted renascence of interest in the Middle Ages, of which the Gothic novel was a part, was, at bottom, a renewal of devotion to those values, structures, and symbols which had been dominant during the medieval epoch.

Behind this rediscovery of the attributes of community, this fascination with community lost and community to be cherished, lies, of course, the perception, the vision, of the masses, of multitudes increasingly disunited, wrenched from the historic contexts of family, village, and religion, without shape, purpose or meaning. A landscape inhabited by atomized individuals rather than by organically connected groups interposing themselves between individual and state: this is the central vision of intellectuals. What Dostoevsky (himself tormented by the demons of modernity) wrote in *The Brothers Karamazov*, in words given to the Grand Inquisitor, is illuminating on the subject of the masses: "For these pitiful beings are concerned not only to find what one or the other can worship, but find something that all will believe and worship; what is essential is that all may be *together* in it. This craving for *community* of worship is the chief misery of man individually and of all humanity from the beginning of time."

Disraeli, in his novel *Sybil*, wrote:

There is no community in England; there is aggregation, but aggregation under circumstances which make it rather a dissociating than a uniting principle. . . . It is community of purpose that constitutes a society. . . . Without that men may be drawn into contiguity, but they will be virtually isolated. . . . In the great cities men are brought together by the desire of gain. They are not in a state of cooperation, but of isolation, as to the making of fortunes; and for all the rest they are careless of neighbors. Christianity teaches us to love our neighbor as ourself; modern society acknowledges no neighbor.

Such words bespeak the view of the social landscape as "mass society," in which Carlyle saw the triumph of "machinery" and the "cash-nexus," and which minds as far apart otherwise as Ruskin and Marx perceived in terms of a proletarianization that, like a plague, must in time destroy the ancient communities which had come down from the Middle Ages.

Yet side by side with envisagement of the forces leading to the masses, to disintegration of historically developed communities, lay, as I have stressed here, perceptions, intimations of a redeeming manifestation of community that might be found in nature, in the tiny village, in contemplation of peasant or laborer, in religion, work, even in revolution. Whether in Wordsworth's *Lyrical Ballads*, Carlyle's *Past and Present*, or Marx's preoccupation with the proletariat, a concern with intimacies and manifestations of community is but the other side of recognition of a landscape dominated by the masses.

Tocqueville is, above any other single writer of the century, the prophet of the mass-age, as J. P. Mayer, our preeminent Tocqueville scholar, pointed out many years ago. The vision of the masses, of their historical rise in modern Western history and their destructive impact upon culture and the nature of the individual, was well fixed in Tocqueville's mind, we realize from his letters and notes, before he made his historic visit to the United States in 1831. He had read the conservative antagonists of the French Revolution, Burke among them, and he had grown up in a Paris dominated by controversy between traditionalists and reactionaries on the one hand and such radical minds as Saint-Simon and Fourier on the other, all alike preoccupied by the masses. Tocqueville's obsession with the "majority" and with "equality" bespeak, as we read him in context, prior obsession with the leveled masses, from which class, local community, and extended family have been stripped, leaving them at one and the same time the root of and the ultimate victims of a new form of despotism, the harshest mankind ever had known or ever would know, Tocqueville thought, in human history. It would be a despotism nurtured in democracy's affinity with mass society, in its emphasis upon majority will and upon egalitarianism, that in due course would extinguish from the individual all desire for, even capacity to endure, genuine liberty.

Not everyone in the century had Tocqueville's tragic sense of the masses. Marx, though possessed of clear vision of the *lumpenproletariat* that would never become a part of the forward movement of history, saw in the working masses the potentialities for creation of a genuine, articulated, well-organized, working *class*, the proletariat, capable of succeeding the capitalist class and of carrying mankind forward to society that would be eventually classless, liberated from private property and profit, that is, socialist. Tolstoy, not a socialist in any sense that would have passed muster with either Marx or most other Western radicals, was obsessed by the masses and their role in history. His *War and Peace*, especially the appendix he affixed to the novel, makes evident his strong belief that the masses, not individuals in their varied roles, govern the movement of history. It was easy for Tolstoy, given his acquired faith in the masses, whether in history or in his own present, to reach virtual adoration of the peasant in his relation to family and land, an adoration that became for a time a cult in Germany and other parts of the West.

For the most part, however, the sense of the landscape as being covered increasingly by the masses, uprooted from community, dislodged from moral code, bereft of authority or organization, is a somber one as we find it in nineteenth-century writing. The sociologists were, as I have noted, far from alone in their premonitions of breakdown resulting from the rise of the masses. From Edmund Burke through Coleridge, Carlyle, Arnold, and Ruskin in England, through Tocqueville, Taine, and Nietzsche on the Continent, down to such minds in our own century as Spengler, Ortega y Gasset, and Hannah Arendt, the vision of the masses has been among the most powerful to emerge from the nineteenth century. Rarely has any intellectual landscape proved more seminal.

POWER

Second, I think, only to the vision of the masses is that of the new contours and hues of *power* which seemed to so many in the century—philosophers, artists, sociologists—dominating among the features of the Western landscape which had been created by the two revolutions. Concern with power and its uses is very old, of course, in Western thought. What else, at bottom, are such works as Plato's *Republic*, Cicero's orations, Machiavelli's *The Prince*, and Hobbes's *Leviathan* concerned with but the structure of political power? The *philosophes* in the eighteenth century were tantalized by the idea of acquiring, and then using, an absolute political power in the name of reason, rights, and justice. But what we find in the nineteenth century is something quite different: the spreading sense among intellectuals of a power greater, more encompassing, more penetrating of mind and spirit, than anything before known in Western history; a type and intensity of power that had been made possible by political and industrial changes in the West. Fear of power and of its capacity to corrupt and paralyze the human will is very great in the nineteenth century, and has to be seen as the other side of the same coin that is inscribed with the veneration of power by nationalists, militarists, and even some revolutionists. Shelley's lines serve as an excellent introduction to a vein of thought, a rendering of the European landscape, that stretches from the Romantics and conservatives at the beginning of the century down to the works of Weber and Simmel at the end:

> Power, like a desolating pestilence,
> Pollutes whate'er it touches; and obedience,
> Bane of all genius, virtue, freedom, truth,
> Makes slaves of men and of the human frame,
> A mechanized automaton.

Carlyle was especially sensitive to the shape and intensity of the power he found associated with the kinds of government which had been brought into existence in Europe either by the French Revolution directly or by the adherence of politicians and statesmen to the model that had been provided by the Revolution and its Bonapartist aftermath. "In all senses, we worship and follow after Power," he wrote, and he made power the essence of "the faith in Mechanism" which is, he goes on, ever "the common refuge of Weakness and blind Discontent." In *Past and Present* he contrasts the age around him with the medieval period as much in terms of the differing systems of authority represented as of the morality, culture, and sense of creative purpose. He uses the hero in his *Heroes and Hero Worship* as the symbol of any culture in which faith in a true social order is crowned by the military, political and religious leaders brought into being. Our own age is lacking utterly in either genuine heroes or in capacity to recognize them if they were to be made manifest. The kind of leadership Weber would refer to as charismatic, a kind Weber found almost totally lacking in the Europe of his day as the result of the bureaucratization of spirit (mechanization, in Carlyle's wording), is much the same as what Carlyle meant by the hero.

It was the memory of the French Revolution, and, emerging from the Revolution, of Napoleon Bonaparte that more than anything else generated both worship and fear of power in the nineteenth century. The Revolution had brought to an apogee, at least in the declarations of its leaders, the conception of power that, rooted deeply in the people it was designed to liberate and reform, would transform the whole of society and even give redemption on earth to mankind. In their successive decrees on family, commune, church, social class, property, and other elements of the traditional social order, the Revolutionary governments between 1790 and the rise of Napoleon quite literally remade the social structure of France and, as the result of advancing Revolutionary armies and of those missionaries of the Revolution who reached even Asia and Latin America, set in operation forces which would in time remake social structures in other parts of the world. What the Revolution embodied in substantial degree and symbolized in the intellectual mind for a century following was the vision of power absolute, collective, rational, and capable of destroying or subordinating everything that stood between it and the individual.

It was Edmund Burke who first identified this novel form of power taking shape in Revolutionary France and spreading first to other parts of Western Europe, then to other parts of the world. To be sure, it was not new patterns of political power alone that Burke was sensitive to. In a great many passages of his book—and of course in some of his notable parliamentary addresses, particularly those concerning the East India Company, which Burke saw as ravaging India's native morality and social structure—Burke flagellates the rising class of "new dealers" as he called it, the class of the new men of quick and speculative wealth, the financiers and businessmen with a vested interest in remaking the landscape.

There were those of both the left and the right to carry on Burke's perceptions. The English radical William Cobbett was nurtured as a youth on Burke's writings, and to the end of his days, though constantly beset by the forces of law and order in England, always in danger of imprisonment, even execution, for his radical doctrines, Cobbett maintained the perfect consistency of his ideas and those he had absorbed from Burke. The conflict Burke had seen between the natural authorities of the people and the artificial, constricting, and repressive powers of government and the new finance was a conflict that Cobbett, along with other radicals, declared fundamental in their speeches and writings.

It was, nevertheless, those of a more conservative cast of mind, such as Coleridge, Southey, Bonald, Haller, Hegel, and Tocqueville, in whom we find the larger evidences of the impact of Burke's intuitions concerning the crisis of authority in the West. Without exception these and a great many other minds were convinced that this crisis was a real one, with effects to be witnessed in culture, scholarship, art, and learning as well as in governments and social orders. The same sensitivity to social landscape that produced Romantic awareness of community produced also awareness of the cataclysmic (as it seemed) change from one kind of overall pattern of authority to another that was fast devouring the natural sources of association and individuality.

"In our days," Tocqueville wrote in 1840 in words reminiscent of Burke, Coleridge, and Southey, "men see that the constituted powers are crumbling down on every side; they see all ancient authority dying out, and the judgment of the wisest is troubled at the sight. . . ." And, also like Burke, Tocqueville saw the source of this erosion of authority in the landscape as the centralized and bureaucratized power of the new national state rooted in the will of the people, or the fiction of the will of the people.

What emerges resplendently in the literary and scientific or philosophical thought of the nineteenth century is the distinction between *authority*—conceived as social and cultural in character, naturally resident in every form of social grouping, and vital to human personality—and *power*, commonly represented in political and military terms. The European landscape is widely painted in terms of the contours of ancient authority existing in a kind of geological tension with upthrusts of the kind of power carried by the soldier, the politician and the bureaucrat. Marx was perfectly well aware of this tension, and refers to it. Unlike Tocqueville, however, Marx paints the political state as but the superstructure for the underlying capitalist class, alone the bearer of absolute power so far as Marx was concerned.

All of this fascination of artist and scholar with power was novel in intensity and breadth. In traditional society authority is hardly recognized as having separate or distinguishable identity, for it is so deeply embedded in functions performed by family, parish, church, and social class as to be virtually unrecognizable. Art is always responsive to crisis, and, as I have emphasized, it was only in the presence of the two great revolutions that the nature of authority became vivid, side by side with the dramatically claimed powers of the new, often revolutionary governments in the West.

Of all sociological landscapists concerned with the patterns of authority, Weber is unquestionably the greatest. He is to this day cited in nearly every systematic treatment of power or authority, and his concept of *rationalization* is if anything more sovereign today in the social sciences than it was in his own time. What Weber saw in the Western Europe before him was the conversion of traditional and personal types of authority into those based upon the rational ends-means schema. A "disenchantment of the world" (a phrase Weber draws from the poet-dramatist Schiller) has taken place in all spheres of life. No longer does ritual or dogma command as it once did; no longer are the native rhythms of nature and society ascendant; human beings have lost their natural resting places in the timeworn authorities of family and local community. In the place of these stands, on ever-widening scale, bureaucracy, which is itself a form of rationalization of human relationships, ends, and means. Not in government alone, but in church, army, education, industry, and recreation, could Weber see the tidal sweep of rationalization of power. Side by side with portrait there existed in Weber's sociology a very distinct, richly hued landscape in which the irresistible erosive effects of rationalization could be seen at every hand.

If it was the artist's vision that first yielded this rendering of the Western European landscape, the works of the empirical researcher were not far behind. There is no real way of "proving" or verifying the vision I speak of, whether expressed in Burke's, Coleridge's, James Thomson's (in *The City of Dreadful Night*), or some of the French Impressionists' terms. No more is there any way, at bottom, of "proving" the truth of Weber's vision of rationalization. All I am saying is that, given the artist's vision in the first place, an army of researchers into fact and circumstance began to form in some of the social sciences, an army that exists to this moment. Beyond number are the studies of this bureaucracy or that, this agency, commission, and office or that, and no one questions the value of such fact-grubbing, whether by academic or government officeholder. But such work would be largely meaningless, I suggest, apart from the inspiriting vision that art alone has given to the foundations of this work.

There is one other manifestation of power on the European landscape in the nineteenth century that should be mentioned here by virtue of the striking appeal it had for artists, philosophers, and sociologists alike. This is, in a word, Bonapartism. What came to be known later in the century as *l'idée napoléonienne* contributed without doubt to Max Weber's characterization of charismatic leadership in politics (the late Leo Strauss wrote that Weber's entire typology of power with its categories of "traditional," "rational," and "charismatic" is a product of response to the French Revolution and the Napoleonic aftermath). The Napoleonic Idea most certainly had its wide appeal to artists, novelists, poets, and dramatists throughout the century. Innumerable are the portraits, with those of Jacques Louis David foremost, of this remarkable man, and it can hardly be doubted that the style of portrait-rendering of Napoleon communicated itself widely in the century with respect to other titans, of politics, war, and industry. In literature, if the novels of Stendhal reveal virtual adoration of Bonapartism, the writings of the Tory traditionalist Walter Scott show a decidedly different reaction, though one not lacking in appreciation of Napoleon's strengths. Romantic art and literature were for a time almost obsessed with Napoleon and the distinctive form of power his years of rule embodied.

It was, though, the sociologists and their forerunners who did the most to analyze and make categorical the Napoleonic Idea. We need go no further back than Tocqueville whose notebooks, as well as fragments left behind at his death which would have gone into the sequel to *The Old Regime and the French Revolution*, produce a vision of Napoleon that proved seminal in the historical, political, and sociological writings of the century. Tocqueville caught the full flavor of personal rule, absolute in quality but designedly rooted deeply in the masses, in popular appreciation, destructive of all intermediate bodies and institutions but compensating for this in the degree to which absolute power was made to seem liberative and also humanitarian to an entire people.

Marx, in his *Eighteenth Brumaire*, which was of course primarily concerned with the Revolution of 1848 and its aftermath culminating in the accession of the second Napoleon, has some highly perceptive observations to make on *l'idée napoléonienne* and emphasizes the attractive contrast it could offer to the thick and omnipresent bureaucracy of the time. Marx saw the extent to which the strength of the second Napoleon, for all the rhetoric about his being representative of the entire people, was in fact grounded in certain powerful elites. But Marx saw too the appeal, or potential appeal, which lay in the structure of this Napoleonic legend, myth, and reality.

Weber was fascinated by the charismatic qualities of this kind of power in its relation to the people, seeing in it, whether in political or religious form, the likeliest antidote to the constricting bureaucracy of the age. Of all the sociologists, though, it is undoubtedly Michels, in his classic study of labor unions, political parties, and other bodies, who best described the Napoleonic Idea. The "iron law of oligarchy" that Michels discerned could easily be developed into the kind of direct, absolute, centralized rule of a single individual. "Once elected," Michels writes, "the chosen of the people can no longer be opposed in any way. He personifies the majority, and all resistance to his will is antidemocratic. . . . One of the consequences of the theory of the popular will being subsumed in the supreme executive is that the elements which intervene between the latter and the former, the public officials, that is to say, must be kept in a state of the strictest possible dependence upon the central authority, which in turn depends upon the people. The least manifestation of liberty on the part of the bureaucracy would be tantamount to a rebellion against the sovereignty of the citizens. . . . Bonapartism does not recognize any intermediate links."

AMONG THESE DARK SATANIC MILLS

Blake's famous line, written in passionate hatred of all that had, in his mind, desolated "England's green and pleasant Land," will serve adequately to epitomize the view of the factory system we find almost everywhere in the intellectual's rendering of the European landscape. With rarest exceptions, artists, philosophers, and sociologists alike in the nineteenth century tended to see the new factory as hateful and as representative of a greater tyranny of body and mind than could be found in any economic order before it.

In actual fact, there is, as a large body of scholarship has made evident during the past two or three decades, much reason to see in the factory system a very considerable improvement of the position of the European worker. From the very Romanticism that flagellated the new structures of industry comes the view of preindustrial Europe as near to rural paradise, a scene of pastoral tranquility and contentment. Not often do we get from the historians and sociologists, and also the artists of the time, the more correct view that contains the untold hardships, torments, oppressions, and degradations attending the life of the great majority of people in the preindustrial scene. Demanding as the new disciplines of work in the machine-driven factories could be, harsh as the rule of overseers might sometimes be on children and women as well as men, it should not be forgotten that women and children worked in rural Europe too, amidst not only manmade disciplines but those of nature, bitterly cold and wet in winter, blazing hot under the summer sun. Living conditions were commonly squalid and disease-ridden, life expectancy short, and the lot of laboring poor in the European countryside, as a host of observers have recorded, was very far from the idyll that began to be constructed by the Romantic mind at the beginning of the nineteenth century.

We live, nevertheless, by images and symbols. And the image of the factory system that began to form in the intellectual mind proved to be a powerful one, lasting down to the present day. It did not matter that in a vast number of instances the new factories were far cleaner, less disease-prone, better sheltered against the elements, with working hours often shorter, than what most of the lower classes had known on the estates and farms of England and France, where work from sunrise until pitch dark was the rule. What did matter was the image of the factory system that almost from the beginning took hold. Blake's "dark, satanic mills" became in effect an entire ideology, found in some degree in the conservative Burke, Coleridge, and Disraeli as well as in the radical minds of the Cobbetts, Blancs, Marxes, from whose writings issued forth a condemnation of the factory and the whole system of property, competition, and profit that accompanied it. Never mind that, as the result of economic growth and the spread of industry, people were living longer lives, eating far better, knowing—with inevitable exceptions of course—better housing on the whole than their forefathers had known in rural slums. The picture, the landscape, that an increasing number of European artists and intellectuals drew in the nineteenth century was commonly harsh, forbidding, bleak, and desolate so far as the economic scene was concerned. Except in style and format, there is little difference to be found between a Dickens and a Marx, a Zola and a Proudhon, in representations of this scene.

I do not want to suggest that the factory system was without defenders. A whole, powerful ideology developed among owners, managers, stockholders, *rentiers*, landlords, as well as among a great many middle-class workers and of course politicians. It would be absurd to imply that the New Materialism, with its vaunted technology, its celebration of the ethic of work, its production of astronomical numbers of consumer goods, its railroads which carried first thousands, then many millions across a continent, and its ships which through steam power brought whole continents close to one another, was devoid of support and applause. There were even writers, such as the remarkable Samuel Smiles, to pen tributes to the new system and to the distinctive virtues required to make it work. Even the working class, especially in the United States, through its trade unions (which Lenin declared to be near-bastions of capitalism), could become ardent defenders of the new capitalist economy, and the middle class reached previously undreamed-of extent and power in society.

But my concern in this book is with sociology; more precisely, with sociological landscapes and portraits. And it has to be admitted that with only occasional exceptions sociologists from Comte to Simmel, Weber, and Durkheim adopted a view of industrialism that was not very different from the one that had first germinated in the minds of the Romantic poets and novelists and essayists. What the art historian Kenneth Clark has written in *Civilisation* on the general subject of what he has called "heroic materialism" is pertinent here. "The early pictures of heavy industry are optimistic. Even the workers didn't object to it because it was hellish but because they were afraid that machinery would put them out of work. The only people who saw through industrialism in those early days were the poets. Blake, as everyone knows, thought that mills were the work of Satan. 'Oh Satan, my youngest born . . . thy work is Eternal Death with Mills and Ovens and Cauldrons.' " Blake was far from alone among Romantic poets. Wordsworth and Burns penned some devastating lines about the mechanizing, brutalizing effects of mechanical industry. Carlyle made "machinery" the very symbol, as we have seen, of the new society he so detested. The Romantics in literature, and also in some degree in painting, really began, in short, the mode of envisagement that, however much it may have been at odds with the way the great majority of people regarded mechanical marvels, proved for the most part to be the lasting mode so far as the minds of artists and intellectuals were concerned. Those painters and poets who were the first to give rendering to the Industrial Revolution almost invariably represented the fires in the iron foundries as the mouth of hell. In France the movement of painting we know as social realism, with Courbet and Millet among its chief representatives, sought with every possible device to do on canvas what such novelists as Mrs. Gaskell, Charles Kingsley, Charles Dickens, and Emile Zola succeeded at in print: to make of the Industrial Revolution something ugly, debasing, brutalizing, and tyrannous to man.

It is thus not suprising that Marx, whose landscapes of capitalism and its works were to prove the dominant ones among intellectuals in the century, should have begun his writing life as a Romantic poet. Bad though Marx's early poems are, they breathe the same fire of revolt against industrial materialism and political oppression that we find in the works of some of the major poets. It is in *Capital*, though, that we find Marx's richest landscape: one in which the poverty of the worker, the inescapable subjection to the machine, the desolating conditions of work in factories, mills and mines, and the ineradicable conflict between proletarian and capitalist are set forth in commanding detail.

But even before Marx wrote *Capital*, before he wrote anything indeed, there were social philosophers and sociologists to set forth their fundamentally hostile representations of what was so widely known as "the Factory System." Saint-Simon, Fourier, and Comte accepted the *idea* of industry—that is, they were not Romantic pastoralists—but they did not accept in any form or degree the industrialism that had first come into being in England at the end of the eighteenth century and was fast-spreading in the France of their day. What was desired was, in Saint-Simon's phrasing, a "New Christianity"; in Fourier's, a system of "phalansteries"; and in Comte's, a Positivist Order, in each of which industry, coupled with the machine, would exist but be stripped of its repressive and brutalizing effects, as these intellectuals perceived them in the industrialism actually regnant. Tocqueville, in the second volume of *Democracy in America*, published in 1840, offers us a grim picture of the "new aristocracy of manufacturers" side by side with a working class that must, by reason of the psychologically destructive effects upon individual workers of the system of division of labor, become ever more degraded. And well before Marx wrote, in *Capital*, his prediction of economic convulsions ever more severe in the capitalist order, Tocqueville, in the volume just referred to, prophesied an endless future in democracy of "recurring commercial panics."

This landscape is to be found also in the sociological writings of Toennies, Weber, Durkheim, and Simmel. It is *Gesellschaft* that, for Toennies, characterizes the economic system of the late nineteenth century: society become increasingly impersonal, contractual, secular, with human beings separated from the organic ties of *Gemeinschaft* that their forebears had known. Weber sees capitalism as but a manifestation of the rationalization, the bureaucratization, of life that was for him the master-process in European modern history. Socialism, for Weber, would be but an intensification of this rationalization. It is industry and the factory system that lie behind the "anomic" or "pathological" forms of division of labor that Durkheim describes in the final part of his first great work, *The Division of Labor*. Much less interested in economic phenomena generally than were Toennies and Weber, Durkheim yet finds industrialism a major factor in generating the kind of weakening of the social bond that breeds rising incidences of suicide in modern life. And for Simmel, industrialism or capitalism represents the triumph of that form of power over individual life which he describes as "objectivism"; the power inherent in things, especially mechanical things, and processes and systems, all brought, in Simmel's view, to a high peak of development in the capitalist system.

Nowhere is the underlying historical unity of sociology and the artistic consciousness of the nineteenth century more vividly displayed, in summary, than in the renderings of the industrial landscape which issue from literature, painting, and sociology alike in that age.

METROPOLIS

So far as landscape is concerned, the city came into its own in the West in the nineteenth century. In painting there were, among others, the Impressionists in France who, as Arnold Hauser has emphasized in *The Social History of Art*, recognized in the city the truly "natural" abode of modern man and who, in their innumerable sketches of public squares, cafes, street corners, city parks, and congested streets, gave to urban life a brilliance of image that had previously been reserved for countryside and village. César Graña has perceptively noted the affinity between the vision of the city given us by the Impressionists and that provided by Simmel in his great essay on metropolis, which I shall come to in a moment. So too was the city a favored setting in the literature of the age, most notably, of course, in the novel. Balzac, Dostoevsky, Dickens, Thackeray, Flaubert, Zola, Stendhal, Gissing: these names chosen at random are sufficient indication of the degree to which urban life and urban social types flourished in the century. Sociology's own interest in the city and in the contrast of city and countryside is very much a part of the larger artistic and philosophical and scientific interest in the city.

In another, more specialized respect, sociology shares something vital with art and literature: a very definite distrust or suspicion of the city, or if that is too strong, a type of perception that tends to see the city not in any serious terms of organic relationships among individuals but instead as a place of largely egoistic, avaricious cunning and of superficial, transitory, and estranged individuals pursuing lives ranging from grim hardship to affluent futility. The pattern that sociology was to give the city in its monographs and essays, best exemplified by the writings of Simmel in Europe and the early University of Chicago sociologists in this country, was well fixed in the literature and art of the nineteenth century before Toennies, Weber, Durkheim, and Simmel wrote any of their works.

Raymond Williams has shown us in a recent work on the contrasting themes of city and countryside in Western writing how deep has been the intellectual's repugnance for the city and its values, for the most part. And, as Morton and Lucia White made clear in a comparable study of the American intellectual, precisely the same repugnance, or at very least distrust, is to be found among Americans, beginning with colonial days. There is very little, we judge, in Western writing on the city that takes the city in the terms of acceptance as a way of life which we find, say, in Asiatic thought over the centuries.

It is strange, as one thinks about it, that the dominant presentation of the city in the West in philosophy and art as well as in the social sciences, should be so negative, so singlemindedly determined to portray it as a place of antisocial and even antihuman settings. For it is impossible to think of any major city in the West— and I include the nineteenth century in this statement—without very real manifestations of community, association, and neighborhood; as real, I would argue, as any to be found in the so-often romanticized rural areas. In America we need think only of the deep ethnic ties which existed among Jews, Germans, Poles, Irish, and others from the very beginning of their settling in such cities as New York, Boston, and Philadelphia. In Europe it was perhaps more likely to be the ties of social class rather than of ethnic strain as such, but the results were the same: a profound sense of human interaction, of rootedness going back oftentimes many generations, and of identity.

In European and American city alike in the nineteenth and early twentieth centuries, the tie of neighborhood was a powerful one. It still is in many places, though it is a rare American in the hinterland who is likely to think of a metropolis like New York as a collection of neighborhoods. Granted that, as the result of ecological changes, chiefly economic, zoning practices, and vast projects in "urban renewal," many neighborhoods have been lost or diminished, they are not gone. In the nineteenth century, certainly, when portrayals of the large city, in works of art and social science, were becoming staples of reading fare, the intensity of neighborhood was, and had to be, very great.

Add to the tie of neighborhood in the large city the bonds provided by such associations, all voluntary, as mutual-aid groups, friendly societies, burial and assurance societies, and cooperatives, and what we see in fact is more nearly a *communitas communitatum* than a mechanical aggregate of isolated individual particles. I am not idealizing the nineteenth- or twentieth-century city. Problems of poverty and housing and violence could be, and often were, great. The economic wretchedness of vast numbers of urban dwellers cannot be disregarded. But I am referring to the *social* image of the city that becomes so widespread in the writing of the nineteenth century, and this is an image not of ties and bonds among people, whether in poverty or affluence, but instead of the utter absence of such ties and bonds. If the negative image of the city in the minds of artists and sociologists of the century were based *solely* upon the undoubted mass of poverty, the case would be a different one, for of the volume of that mass there can be no question. But the essential point is that accompanying, often even overriding, the sense of the city as a place of impoverishment, is the sense of the city as the reservoir of isolated, estranged, alienated, and psychologically insecure individuals. It is this view, rather than a strictly economic one, that takes foremost place in the sociological mind in the century, reaching, as I have noted, its high point in the writings of Simmel, whose perspective so quickly reached the United States and became the basis of the very distinctive sociology that emerged from the University of Chicago early in the twentieth century.

Behind the sociologist's landscape of the city as a place of teeming, estranged, and unhappy masses lies the earlier one composed by the Romantics of the late eighteenth and early nineteenth centuries. We have Rousseau's *Confessions* to mark, if not the beginning, then the secure fixing of the Romantic view. Rousseau hated Paris, the city in which so much of his life was spent, and the final pages of the *Confessions* make evident enough his contempt for urban life and his declared love of rural tranquility where alone true virtue may be found. There is no significant exception, so far as I know, in Romantic writing of the early nineteenth century to this sense of the superior moral and social worth of the pastoral and rural to the urban. Insensibly there emerges from poem, essay, and tract the vision of the city as the abode of not only the criminal but the tormented.

This is the time when the adverse reaction to crowds becomes manifest in European writing. The fact that the vast majority of those living in large cities seem actually to like, to be, indeed, psychologically dependent upon, the physical closeness of others, had no effect upon the Romantic mind. What began to be known as "teeming masses" obsessed those for whom the new city was a symbol of the triumph of modernity over the values of traditionalism. Repeatedly, in the writings of Carlyle, Morris, Ruskin, and others, the contemporary city is contrasted with the medieval town, above all with the rural village, and high among the evil attributes which are given a London or Paris or Rome by the Romantics is the sheer number of people. The landscape of the masses becomes fused, in short, with that of the city. That there were rural masses, so often plunged into desolating poverty of mind as well as purse, whose only relief, as John Wesley discovered and made the basis of the social appeal of Methodism, was religious revivalism, seems never to have occurred to the Romantic poets and essayists of the time. With rare exceptions, rural equaled good, urban equaled evil. "The City is of Night; perchance of Death,/But certainly of Night," wrote James Thomson in *The City of Dreadful Night*, and although reference to city is in substantial degree metaphoric, covering all of modernity, there can be no doubt of Thomson's feelings about the large city itself.

If there is a single literary sentence that may be said to have generated the quintessential sociological view of the city, it is one by Charles Caleb Colton, who died in 1832. It is to be found in his *Lacon:* "If you would be known and not know, vegetate in a village; if you would know, and not be known, live in a city." This is more germinal than, say, Wordsworth's "dissolute city" or Dickens' "the city is barren," for in it lies the contrast that sociologists would make central: the envisagement of the village or rural as a setting of individual dullness but of community; of the city as the setting of individual acuity but absence of community.

Fundamentally, that is the theme of Simmel's masterpiece, *Metropolis and Mental Life*, the work, as I have said, that above any other established securely the landscape of city that has predominated in sociological writing almost to the present moment. For Simmel—who, it should be noted, seems to have lived happily and with the closest of friends in urban context—the city is the preserve of the egoistic, the separated, the estranged, the purely calculating, and, above all the reserved, mind. The city, Simmel tells us, puts a high premium upon individual reserve, holding back one's emotional capital, whether in sadness or joy, and upon relationships which are of role only, that is, as buyers and sellers, employers and employees, fellow-riders of the tram or subway, and so on. The mind prospers, becomes ever more acute, sensitive, and perceptive in the city, but the spirit, the soul, tends to become warped, the consequence of its isolation from the "organic" ties which are to be found only in the village or small town. Overwhelmingly the city is the refuge of the "sharp dealer," the individual on the make, the person who devotes himself to living, as it were, on the fringes of law and morality. It is every man for himself, the jungle, the rat-race, and, not least, the means of quick if impermanent success, especially financial success.

No one will question the fact that the city, any city, *is* all of this. Landscapes which highlight these attributes are indeed possible. But, as I have noted, the city is, and always has been, a great deal else too: solidarity of neighborhood, ethnic group, mutual-aid association, extended family, club, tavern, feast-day, and much more. Granted that there are lonely individuals in the city; so are there in the small town and village. There are also to be found in the city large numbers for whom the absence of the essential traits of the rural village permits a form of creative freedom that is by no means incompatible with the sense of community.

So much is true. But the landscape of metropolis that had become securely established in sociology by the beginning of the present century takes little account of anything but the qualities which the Romantics had identified a century earlier and which had then become the stock-in-trade of poets, novelists, dramatists, and painters throughout the century. It is a sociological landscape done most brilliantly by Simmel but by no means done alone; the same basic image of the city, the same lights, shadows, and contours are to be found in the writings of Weber, Toennies, and Durkheim—and, as I have said, in the large number of monographs which emerged from the University of Chicago starting about 1910.

Just as a literary vision was the germination of a perspective that in time became a staple of sociology, so did sociological insight contribute in return to literature. For there is a great deal more than coincidence in the fact that the same city of Chicago in which we find sociologists like W. I. Thomas and Robert Park is the one which we find the subject of novelists like Herrick, Dreiser, and in time Farrell and Algren. If one desires a rendering of urban landscape as this has become fixed in sociology, he can as easily obtain it from such novels as *The Titan* (Dreiser) and *The Common Lot*

(Herrick) as from any of the works of the sociologists of the University of Chicago. Nor should we forget the urban landscape depicted by poets such as Sandburg, Masters, and Lindsay during the period. It too is sociological to the core. I have stressed in this book the fact that sociology is an art form, drawing inspiration from the same basic sources as literature and painting in the nineteenth century. But with equal truth we can describe a great deal of literature and other art of the age as imaginative forms of sociology. This is true of Dickens's London, Proust's Paris, and Dreiser's Chicago as it is of certain lithographs by Doré, Daumier, and Géricault and of paintings by the Impressionists and Naturalists, along with other artistic expressions of what Kenneth Clark has referred to as Heroic Materialism.

4

Sociological Portraits

The portrait too is a major form of sociological expression in the nineteenth century, though not often did the sociologists chiefly responsible, such as Marx and Weber, regard themselves as belonging to this genre. Suffice it to say that the portraits which do emerge from sociological writing—the *bourgeois*, the *worker*, the *bureaucrat*, and the *intellectual*, for example, which are the ones I shall deal with in this section—can easily take their places with the work of artists like Millet and Daumier and with the memorable political and economic portraits given us by such novelists as Dickens, Kingsley, Thackeray, and others.

The nineteenth century is one of the ages—Alexandrian Greece, the Rome of the Caesars, the modern Renaissance, are others—in which the portrait, whether in words, in marble, or on canvas, became an especially prized form of art. Behind the burst of portraiture in such ages is the eruption of large numbers of distinctive individuals, or, rather, of individual *role-types:* politicians, diplomats, soldiers, financiers, businessmen, artists, and scientists. Not only great individuals but reigning families become conspicuous in the portraits of such ages, and the desire for portraiture can be as great among the writers and artists who compose them as among the individuals who are subjects. A great many museums in the West attest today to the recurrent impulse in Western history to make individuals and families somewhat larger than life, but also to fuse them, by expert design, into the life of their age, to endow them, in short, with historicity as well as individuality.

It may be said that portraits done by the artist are more likely to emphasize individual characteristics—attributes unique to a given human being—whereas the portraits which come from sociology are more given to emphasizing traits which large numbers of individuals in a certain class or occupation exhibit commonly. Nevertheless, it is well to remember that the artist, painter, or novelist seeks more than faithful duplication of the individual he is describing. Thus, it should not be imagined that Rembrandt's *Portrait of a Rabbi* or Frans Hals's *Descartes* is only what each is labeled. No one can miss in the Rembrandt the artist's desire to limn a contemporary role that attracted him, irrespective of the specific individual actually painted. And Hals's *Descartes*, exact though it may be in its portrait of an actual philosopher, exemplifies a general type, a profoundly honored type, in the Europe of the seventeenth century. In Dostoevsky's *Crime and Punishment*, based upon his own experiences with police and prison, Raskolnikov is not only a highly memorable individual but also the image of a class or type Dostoevsky was fascinated by: the revolutionary nihilist of his time. And yet, this said, it remains true that the difference between the kinds of portraits we find in the arts and those which I shall be concerned with in this chapter, drawn from sociology, is essentially the higher degree of attention paid by the arts to individuality, to qualities intended to be and to seem unique in the subject, for in sociological writing a certain level of abstraction and generalization is inescapable.

There is nothing astonishing in the fact that clearly etched portraits emerge from the writings of Marx, Weber, and others. The nineteenth century was, as I have noted, an age unusually rich in portraits which reveal the political and economic values of the period. Historical writing, that of such minds as Ranke, Michelet, Macaulay, and many others, is filled with memorable portraits of figures of the past. Mommsen's characterization of Julius Caesar was based, as we know, upon his own artist-historian's reaction to his contemporary Bismarck. Biographies and autobiographies were written and published by the hundreds in all Western countries. Not before or since has the biographer's art been as popular as it was in book and magazine in the nineteenth century. The same is true of portraits painted. Beyond count are the renderings of notables in politics, war, finance, and trade.

Equally striking are the portraits in the novels and short stories and dramas of the period. It is hard to believe that any century in history has, in its imaginative writing, created so many lasting personages, so many vivid human symbols of mood, time, place, and character. From Dostoevsky's Brothers Karamazov or Raskolnikov in *Crime and Punishment* and Tolstoy's Anna Karenina all the way across the continent to Balzac's Père Goriot, Stendhal's Julien Sorel in *The Red and the Black*, and Flaubert's Madame Bovary in France and, in England, Dickens's David Copperfield, Thackeray's Becky Sharp in *Vanity Fair*, Gissing's Biffen in *New Grub Street*, Hardy's Tess of the D'Urbervilles, and Meredith's Richard Feverel, the portraits are memorable. Across the Atlantic were to be found Mark Twain's great Huck Finn and Tom Sawyer and such powerful, if lesser known, portraits as Stephen Crane's Maggie and Howells's Silas Lapham.

Clearly in each of these, and in the many more not here mentioned who fill nineteenth-century novels, we are dealing with a distinct, unforgettable *individual*. It would be wrong to declare that the primary motive of any of the novelists was to give expression to a social type or to personify directly some social condition or image. But it would be equally wrong to deny that Dickens, Dostoevsky, or Mark Twain each had some recognition of the kind of society he was living in, some considerable insight into the kinds of people who exploited or were exploited, who suffered, enjoyed, loved, and hated, and a profound sense of the degree to which, following Hegel's phrase, the universal can exist in the concrete. When Gissing wrote *New Grub Street* he certainly wanted the world to know what the role of the starving writer was in London; Dostoevsky surely composed Raskolnikov out of numerous revolutionists he had known while serving in prison; and we know that for Mark Twain, Huck Finn was the fusion of countless Mississippi River types and experiences he had himself known from boyhood on. In sum, we grant to the literary artist primary concern with individual character rather than with abstract social role or type, but we do not dismiss either the appeal to readers which lies in the fact that a Madame Bovary, a Mr. Bounderby, or a Julien Sorel each represents a significant and pervasive type in the social order. It is no wonder, reading this or that novel from Balzac's *La Comédie humaine*, that Marx should have found Balzac not only excellent reading but also first-rate social documentation. There are individuals in Balzac, yes, but there are also imperious social types: the same social types which populate the pages of sociology in the century.

When we turn to sociology, we are in the presence of portraits—of *role-types*. The concept of social role is, fundamentally, the response made by sociology in the nineteenth century to the problem posed to artists, philosophers, and social scientists by the necessity of somehow imposing an interpretative pattern or structure on eruptive individualism. At the end of the nineteenth century Weber would advance the concept of "ideal-type," applying it equally to structures, processes, and personages. Whether we refer to role-type or ideal-type, the idea is the same: the object, whether structure or personage, stripped, so to speak, of all that is merely superficial and ephemeral, with only what is central and unifying left. Precisely as there is an ideal-type of the human heart or lung—one that no actual, concrete heart or lung exemplifies in every detail—in every textbook in physiology, so is there, or at least so can there be, an ideal-type of bourgeois, soldier, intellectual, or bureaucrat. No living, performing individual in any of these categories will be *exactly* like the description supplied by the sociologist for his ideal-type, but the relation will be nonetheless sufficiently close to give clarifying value to the ideal-type.

Ideal-types, or role-types, as we prefer, are sociological portraits, and irrespective of end they are, and have to be, done with an artist's skill. In the nineteenth century a number of vivid role-types emerged in sociology, and, looking back on them today, we can declare them fit company for the kinds of portraits which were present in the novel, the drama, and the works of painters.

THE BOURGEOIS

Mention the word and the name of Karl Marx springs instantly to mind. Nor is there anything extraordinary about this, for no one who has ever read *The Communist Manifesto* is likely to forget the portrait of the bourgeois, of the bourgeoisie, indeed, in that historic tract. No apologist or propagandist for the new industrial system outdid Marx and Engels in their eulogy to the accomplishments in the modern world of the bourgeoisie, a class destined, however, for all its industrial and technological achievements, to extinction by reason of the contradictions which Marx believed fatal to capitalism. And in eulogizing, in giving last rites, as it were, to the bourgeoisie, Marx created a portrait that has survived to this day.

Not that Marx was alone in his awareness of the bourgeois—the capitalist, the financier, the individual who subordinated everything—family, religion, love, and honor included—to the demands of money and of the whole system of production that was spreading so rapidly. As early as 1790 we have a portrait of the new economic type in Burke's *Reflections on the Revolution in France*, and it is one etched indeed in acid, for Burke despised the new class of "money grubbers" and "new dealers" whose inexhaustible lust for financial gain, as Burke saw it, was destroying a social order he loved, one which, descended from the Middle Ages, was based on land, religion, kinship, and, above all, honor and fealty. It was the triumph of the new industrial class in France that Burke thought to be one of the worst aspects of the Revolution, but, as he is careful to make plain, this class was achieving dominance also in England and elsewhere in the West.

It was Burke, and after him such conservatives as Southey, Coleridge, and Carlyle, in England, who did the most to draw attention to the bourgeoisie—as the class came increasingly to be known first in France, then in all of intellectual Europe—but it was not long before preoccupation with the bourgeois, with the capitalist mind and spirit, became widespread in the literature, philosophy, painting, and social thought of the nineteenth century. Many are the portraits still to be seen on the walls of European galleries, done by classicists, Impressionists, and others through the century, which indicate, sometimes in caricature born of hostility, the impact that was being made by the bourgeois. So too, in the essays of a great many philosophical and literary observers of the scene in the century—Chateaubriand, Sainte-Beuve, Carlyle, and Matthew Arnold, among others—is the portrait, commonly hostile, of the bourgeois, the man of economic soul, to be found. And the bourgeois inhabits a great many of the novels of the age, among them those of Mrs. Gaskell, Charles Kingsley, Thomas Love Peacock—and Dickens!

Dickens gives us in *Hard Times* (1854) a picture of the capitalist not much different from Marx's. His Thomas Gradgrind and Josiah Bounderby, particularly the latter, are among the most arresting portraits produced by the Industrial Revolution. Gradgrind epitomizes the hard, heartless spirit of pragmatic efficiency, of the suzerainty of the utilitarian in Western culture, that characterized the bourgeoisie. Bounderby is the personification of the rough, aggressive money-maker, the exploiter of human beings, and if Dickens also depicts Bounderby as a liar and scoundrel on all counts, it has to be admitted that Dickens does a good job of making all these qualities seem organically related in his fictional creation. The "cash-nexus" that Carlyle identified and declared pivotal in the society around him has every bit as much reality in Dickens's mind as in Carlyle's.

Or Marx's. No matter how widespread among philosophers and artists in the century the negative image of the capitalist may have been, it is, of course, to Karl Marx that we go for the classic portrait. Just by virtue of the fact that capitalism—with its foundations in the economics of private property and private profit and its division of society into the two major classes, capitalists and wage-earners—is for Marx the major reality of the age, the person of the capitalist is inevitably of transcending importance. As Marx himself explains in the Introduction to *Capital*, he is not concerned with actual human beings, as he would be were he engaged in mere descriptive history. He gives us, by his own account, "personifications of economic categories, embodiments of particular class relations and class interests."

Not that, for Marx, the capitalist is, by any standard, a villain. We never draw from Marx, in his representation of the capitalist system he not only disliked but believed already moribund where it had assumed prominence, the kind of portrayal that came from others in his age, a portrayal of men devoured by their own avarice, cupidity, and desire to exploit. Marx's sociology and his philosophy of history led him to see human beings as inevitably strongly conditioned, even shaped, by the class relations in which they were individual participants. I am not implying that for Marx human beings are but passive, helpless atoms; there is a very real sense in Marx of the individual as active participant in the making of history. Even so, Marx's portrait of the bourgeois capitalist is singularly lacking in the kind of rancor that we see in some of the conservatives of the age, such as Carlyle, Disraeli, and Ruskin.

After all, in *The Communist Manifesto* Marx and Engels had given to the bourgeoisie as a class praise of highest order. Nothing in the ancient world, not one of the so-called seven wonders of the world, equaled in either immensity or sheer constructiveness the works of the bourgeoisie in modern times. These works include the liberation of countless human beings from the "idiocy of rural life," the establishment of trade routes which brought all parts of the world into contact, the creation of technology that had all the potentialities of emancipating human beings from the drudgery that had been their lot for countless millennia, the building of great cities and industries, and a raising of the material standard of life. It is capitalism, Marx tells us, that has formed the basic technological structures which will continue after capitalism itself has been destroyed by its own contradictions, which will continue into the post-capitalist period of socialism, then communism.

For all that, the portrait of the capitalist that shines through in Marx's writing, beginning with his earliest essays and continuing through the works of his mature period, is a harsh one, made so by the interests of the role the capitalist is obliged to fill in the capitalist economy. We see a portrait composed of features repellent in Marx's mind, just as they were in the minds of so many of Marx's intellectual contemporaries: iron self-interest, economic calculation, subordination of all ethical, esthetic, and religious considerations to the one controlling consideration of profit, of the protection of "surplus value," and the inexorable exploitativeness that private property enjoins. That there is also to be seen in Marx's portrait of the capitalist a decided strength of character is not to be denied; after all, in Marx's telling, the capitalist had been able to sweep aside aristocrat, statesman, priest, and soldier to assume command of the historical situation, and that could not have been accomplished by a weakling. But there is to be seen too, if one looks carefully enough at the portrait, premonition of eventual death in the features, a death that was to be the central element of the final act of the whole drama of human history.

That, for all the compelling quality of the Marxian portrait—a portrait, as I have noted, remarkably like others drawn in the age of novelists and painters—there is proved to be, on the historical record, little verisimilitude in the portrait when one looks at the detailed lives of actual businessmen, proprietors, owners, and others of the bourgeoisie in Marx's age and our own does not really matter. Never mind that overwhelmingly in the actual lives of individuals considerations other than self-interest frequently take control, or that the history of the past century is unparalleled in the growth and spread of securities, freedoms, and material comforts to the ever-enlarging middle class and also in the spread of political power to the people. Never mind, in sum, that capitalism in practice has

borne little relationship to the system so eloquently described by
Marx. We live in a world of ideas, and ideas, stereotypes, images
have far greater directive forces in our lives, generally, than do the
conditions they are supposed to reflect. Men, wrote Cardinal Newman, will die for a dogma (say symbol as well) who will not even
stir for a mere conclusion.

The Marxian portrait of the bourgeois has proved to possess
verisimilitude for countless millions. True, Marx was, as I have
said, far from alone in his portraiture. Even Tocqueville gives us a
harsh, at times bitter, picture of individuals, of an entire class,
dominated by greed for money, willing to flout all values and pie-
ties for economic advantage. The class of manufacturers, Tocqueville tells us in *Democracy in America,* is the most predatory of all
upper classes in Western history. But despite the Tocquevilles,
Balzacs, Carlyles, and others who painted portraits of the bourgeoisie in the nineteenth century, it is, without question, Marx who is
most deeply identified with the subject. It has been through Marx's
rendering that the image of the bourgeois has become so powerful
among intellectuals, generally, as we know, with adversary intent
toward the image. To this moment, to describe anyone as
bourgeois in tastes, or in anything, for that matter, is to create an
instant picture of a whole style of life, an entire pattern of attributes, based upon the Marxian thesis of individuals holding roles
which demand subordination of all values to economic interest.

One other portraitist of the capitalist or bourgeois among sociologists deserves mention here: Max Weber. I refer, of course, to his
study of the influence of the Protestant, or Puritan, ethic upon the
rise of capitalism in the sixteenth century in the West. Had it not
been for the Puritan ethic of work, making work a form of prayer,
of service to God, and the endowment of wealth and material possession with the attributes of divine grace, Weber argued, it is unlikely that capitalism would have come into being precisely as it
did.

What we have here, however, is more than historical or causal
explanation. It is, at bottom, a portrait of the quintessential capital-

ist or bourgeois: a being driven, in Weber's terms, not just by desire for wealth, which is an old desire, nor by impulse to dominate and accumulate, which is also old, but rather by the conviction that in the making of great fortunes, in the consecration to business, finance, and to job, one was actually doing God's work, earning, in the first John D. Rockefeller's phrase, "God's gold." Thus to the lineaments of the bourgeois we get from a Marx, or even a Tocqueville, there can be added, in Weber's view, the further lines which reveal on the bourgeois face a certain spirituality, most certainly of austerity, the result of doing, through finance and business, what God wills.

THE WORKER

We must give credit to Marx too for another momentous portrait, equally powerful in evocative quality: that of the worker or proletarian. Again, as with respect to the bourgeois, there were many in the nineteenth century to paint, etch, mold, and describe in words the worker, the industrial worker. But it is Marx's portrait—no less artistic in its selective character than Marx's portrait of the capitalist—that has proved to be dominant and certainly the most universal.

William Empson, the literary scholar, in a study of "types of pastoralism" a generation ago, observed that much the same kind of romantic fixation attended the industrial worker in the nineteenth century as had been given by artists and intellectuals to shepherds or plowboys in an earlier literature in the West as a part of the larger romanticization that included the child and also the "happy savage" of the South Seas and other undeveloped parts of the world. And this was in many ways very different from what we observe in the epics, ballads, dramas, and essays of earlier centuries. It is no exaggeration, I think, to say that from the Greeks down until the eighteenth century references to the worker—that is, the menial, even the craftsman—were, with few exceptions, cast in terms of disdain or caricature. Romantic pastoralism might include the shepherd or plowman, but nothing equivalent existed for the ordinary worker, rural or urban. And even in the eighteenth century a Rousseau's reference to the virtue that might be found under "the homespun of the laborer" was somewhat exceptional. It suffices to say that in this century there was at least the beginning of awareness of the plight of the poor and menial in life. But that is about all.

All of this changed substantially in the nineteenth century. In the first place, as the intellectual historian Gertrude Himmelfarb has pointed out valuably, there was the discovery of the *idea* of poverty. There was of course nothing new in poverty as such; in fact, as I have already suggested, there is considerable ground for believing that the poverty of the nineteenth century was a good deal less in scope and harshness than it had been in earlier centuries. Machinery and rising standards of nutrition, housing, and public welfare accomplished this. But things are as they are perceived. And irrespective of actual, substantive conditions, there appeared, for the first time in Western thought in any significant degree, as Himmelfarb has stressed, a widening awareness of, indeed a preoccupation with, poverty by intellectuals and reformers.

Inevitably Romanticism was involved in this awareness and preoccupation. Marx himself, as his biographers have stressed, began his intellectual life as a Romantic; he had been deeply influenced by the works of Schiller. His earliest work, both in essay and poetic form, reveals what is without question a Romantic view of human nature, and this view persisted into Marx's later writings on capitalism and the position of the working class, as it did too in the works of Marx's associate Friedrich Engels, who had studied the English working class well before his liaison with Marx commenced in the mid-1840s.

But Marx was not alone in his Romantic appreciation of the industrial worker. Before he wrote a line, there were those in England, France, Germany, and elsewhere, including Russia, to endow the worker, rural and urban, with a meaning and dignity not before seen in Western writing. There was, from the very beginning of the nineteenth century in Western society, a distinct confluence of literary and philosophical Romanticism on the one hand and religious and secular humanitarianism on the other; a confluence that has to be reckoned with when we seek to explain the tides of political and economic revolution in the nineteenth and twentieth centuries. As the late Joseph Schumpeter emphasized, the same capitalism that in a real sense created the modern intellectual also created in the intellectual a sense of alienation that ranged from distrust to actual hatred of this economic system.

The "dark satanic mills" the poet-artist Blake wrote about gradually communicated themselves to those interested in the creation of sociology. There is a distinct awareness of the working class in the writings of all the sociologists, Comte, Tocqueville, and even Frederick Le Play included. If I stress the last-named it is solely because he was very much an economic conservative, believed strongly in private property, and thought the factory, when appropriately managed and related to social order, an inevitable part of the future. It was, nevertheless, Le Play who produced, in his *European Working Classes*, the first systematic study of the subject, on a comparative basis, in the century. Quantitative in his method though he assuredly was, the portraits of working-class families we find filling the several large volumes of that work are sociological analogues of the kinds of portraits we find in the imaginative literature and the revolutionary art of the period. For all his conservatism, Le Play made the worker the central figure of his sociological thought; and even earlier, when Le Play was a mining engineer teaching in his spare time in one of the trade schools, he was given regularly to asking each entering class, "What is the most valuable thing to come out of the mine?" and answering his question with, "The worker."

In short, then, the image of the worker gradually became converted to that of an individual not only oppressed and exploited inhumanely but also possessed of a dignity, a worthiness, an underlying wisdom, and, in due time, a favored place in history. That workers in the mills and peasants in the fields had emotions and passions, capacities for love and devotion, manifestations of loyalty, honor, and rectitude, that their lives could contain all the elements of either the pathos or the tragedy that had once been found in the upper classes alone, all of this came as a surprise to a great many readers and observers of art in the nineteenth century. It was not by any means overwhelming in either mass or suddenness, this novel impact of the worker upon the nineteenth-century middle- and upper-class consciousness. But the fact is that the image of the exploited, oppressed, and beleaguered worker became common by the end of the century, the rock on which the so-called proletarian literature was to be founded.

In the nineteenth century there was no explicit concept of proletarian literature as there was to be in the twentieth. All the same, a great deal that was written in the century about industrial workers fits very well indeed into the category. I have mentioned the novels of Dickens, Mrs. Gaskell, and Charles Kingsley, all of which describe city life in the bleakest of terms so far as the poor and oppressed were concerned. In France there was Victor Hugo's *Les Miserables* and, not to be missed, Zola's novels. In such works as *L'Assommoir* and *Germinal*, the lives of workers are described in relentless detail, and there are none of the offsetting scenes of humor that a Dickens will provide in even such a work as *Hard Times, Oliver Twist* or, of course, *David Copperfield*. It was exactly in this tradition that, in the United States at the beginning of the twentieth century, Upton Sinclair wrote his now historic *The Jungle*, in which the lives of slaughter-house workers in Chicago were described in such unrelieved terms of squalor and filth, as well as of hardship and exploitation, that an aroused American citizenry brought about the first federal laws concerning the manufacture of food. No one will doubt that such conditions did exist—and do still exist—in Western working classes, but they are hardly the whole story; not by any means.

As I noted above, there is much hard evidence to support the view that, Romantic nostalgia aside, the condition of the masses of workers was significantly better in the industrial areas of the West in the nineteenth century than it had been for their rural forebears. The statistics on increased life-expectancy, steady improvement of quality of food, lodging, and public sanitation, and, perhaps most significant, on the massive increase of the middle class throughout Western society, all reveal a picture that is very different from the one we associate with the essays of Carlyle and Coleridge, the novels of Dickens and Kingsley, the sketches of Daumier, and, above all, the writings of those such as Proudhon, Blanqui, Bakunin, and Marx, who were in the vanguard of revolutionary opposition to the new economy.

With rare exceptions, as in the work of Le Play, sociology in the nineteenth century falls squarely in the intellectual tradition that had begun with Blake and other Romantic enemies of industrialism. Just as the characteristic landscape in the sociology of the age is constructed in terms of the bleakness, squalor, degradation, and oppression of the system, so is the characteristic portrait of the worker. Between art and sociology, in short, there was a close correspondence of themes when it came to rendering the age and its types. What a Marx or Proudhon conveyed in socialist or sociological writing was conveyed with almost equal effect by painter and poet. We know what an effect Millet's *The Gleaners* could have, how moving for vast numbers of people were the portraits of workers which are found in the novels of the realists and naturalists of the period, what an impact was registered, for example, by Edwin Markham's poem "The Man with a Hoe," itself engendered by one of Millet's works.

What Marx did was infuse into the portrait of the worker the intimation of destiny, of the worker holding as vital a place in the great tide of history as had been held earlier by the master, soldier, nobleman, and, in Marx's own day, the capitalist. In the lineaments of the worker's face as drawn by a Marx is to be found the sense of security that comes from knowledge that through the processes of history already at work will come eventually liberation from toil and entry into the realm of true history. Enslaved by man and machine, exploited by the profit system, reduced to subsistence level, alienated from his work, victim of the fetishism of commodities: such is the portrait of the worker—in defiance of all, or most, empirical reality in the age—that, as drawn by a Marx, could have the eventual effect of changing the very course of history. In this portrait, as in his portrait of the capitalist, Marx created an image that continues to this day to exert the kind of appeal to consciousness that can only come from religion and art.

THE BUREAUCRAT

Weber is, of course, the master artist when it comes to the portrait of the bureaucrat. Again, as with respect to Marx's capitalist and worker, the portrait may be in many respects at variance with what the actual lives of countless human beings reveal statistically, but there is nevertheless sufficient truth, sufficient verisimilitude, to have made Weber's portrait a lasting one in the literature of sociology and also in the wider expanses of writing on society and government.

Not that Weber was the only sociologist or social philosopher to concern himself with this figure. We are indebted to Marx for some of the most perceptive, and also hostile, sketches, especially in *The Eighteenth Brumaire*, of the bureaucrat and of the toils in which he enmeshes the social order. Edmund Burke had delivered himself of lacerating characterizations of the governmental bureaucrat and his obsession with "arbitrary power" in a few of his Parliamentary comments on the British East India Company and its depredations in India. So also, in *Reflections on the Revolution in France*, did Burke address himself to the influence of bureaucracy, especially with respect to its passion for "geometric symmetry," its indifference to social and cultural traditions among a people, its ruthlessness in riding roughshod over the habits and desires of neighborhoods and communities. What Burke has to say about the French bureaucratic passion for unity and homogeneity in the social order, as he saw this passion unfold during the earliest stages of the French Revolution, makes highly pertinent reading even today.

Tocqueville was also fascinated by the appearance in modern history of the bureaucrat, and tells us in *Democracy in America* that one may even trace the progress or advance of mass government, of equalitarian democracy, by the rate of increase in the number of paid servants of the state, that is, bureaucrats. Long before Weber, Tocqueville saw the rising tension in democracy caused by the democracy's spawning of bureaucracy coupled with the constricting effect this very bureaucracy can have upon grass-roots, popular manifestations of opinion. No one has ever exceeded Tocqueville in the power of his characterization of the inherent despotism of the bureaucracy in the future in the West. He writes an entire chapter toward the end of his classic on American democracy on "the kind of despotism democratic peoples have to fear," and this despotism is, of course, that of bureaucracy spread throughout entire populations.

Among novelists in the century there was widening appreciation of the inroads being made by the bureaucrat. Disraeli's novels *Coningsby*, *Sybil*, and *Tancred* are most commonly dealt with in terms of the shattering of the social equilibrium that, in Disraeli's mind, had once characterized English government and society. This is understandable enough, for without question that shattering bulked large in Disraeli's mind. But he would not have been the artist he was had he not drawn upon the resources given him by lifelong fascination with politics and government, and we see in his novels—no doubt in large part as a result of Carlyle's influence on him—distinct and memorable characterizations of civil servants as well as politicians. In what Carlyle had called "the worship of Machinery," Disraeli, like his mentor, could see the suffocating effects upon human lives and communities of the ever-widening hold of officialdom upon society. Nor was Dickens lacking in response to the phenomenon. His often savage attacks upon the official, respectable scene around him included biting caricatures of the operation of the judicial system and its endless pettifogging, its mesh of fine rules and procedures which the finest minds and worthiest cases could not easily break through. And in a number of novels are to be found sketches of the bureaucratic mentality, ranging from the harsh light in which this mentality is shown in the public institution to which the young Oliver Twist is sent by the law all the way to the portrait of Thomas Gradgrind (inspired in such large part by the Bentham-born bureaucratic proposals of Edwin Chadwick), the very epitome of the calculating, utilitarian, rule-forming, and system-dwelling bureaucrat.

There was thus a very considerable background of response to the "new despotism" which so many, from the ideological left as well as right, saw in the spreading bureaucracy when Max Weber came to write his many pages on the subject of bureaucracy and his portrait of the bureaucrat. No more than Marx does Weber seek to make a villain of his central personage. "The individual bureaucrat," Weber writes, "cannot squirm out of the apparatus in which he is harnessed." Just as Marx's capitalist is the product of his class and the profit system on which it rests, so Weber's bureaucrat is the product of the rising utilization of the expert in matters of administration. Nor is the bureaucrat that Weber limns for us confined to official government alone. He is to be seen increasingly in education, the military, and religion, thus creating a widening void between human beings and the basic functions of the social order.

What emerges in Weber's portrait of the bureaucrat is a being conceived in the application of pure reason—joyless, emotionless reason—to human affairs. "In contrast to the honorific or avocational notable, the professional bureaucrat is chained to his activity by his entire material and ideal existence. In the great majority of cases, he is only a single cog in an ever-moving mechanism which prescribes to him a fixed route of march." There is more than a hint of tragedy in Weber's portrait. For if it is an honored value, reason, that is the rock on which bureaucracy is built, if it is understandable worship of expertise in a given line that leads to replacement of amateur by professional, still reason and expertise are the qualities which in the long run make for the bureaucrat's increasingly authoritarian hold upon the social order and his increasingly suffocating effect on the human mind and spirit. If Comte had seen individualism as the disease of the Western World, the passage of a few decades made it possible for Weber to define this disease as bureaucracy instead.

Nor are the widely favored solutions of socialism and communism in any way appealing to Weber. In each he sees the bureaucrat as assuming even greater power and influence than in capitalism. For Weber the bureaucrat is, without question, the preeminent figure in the world of today and of the foreseeable future. In his final years Weber became pessimistic in the extreme. "It is horrible to think that the world could one day be filled with nothing but those little cogs, little men clinging to little jobs and striving towards bigger ones. . . . That the world should know no men but these: . . . and the great question is, therefore . . . what we can oppose to this machinery in order to keep a portion of mankind free from this parceling-out of the soul, from this supreme mastery of the bureaucratic way of life."

No more than Marx's capitalist or worker is Weber's bureaucrat the empirically exact representation of each and every civil servant or governmental employee. It is unlikely indeed that any bureaucratic office could operate very long if its inhabitants answered precisely to the portrait of the bureaucrat that is given us by Weber and subsequently by Michels, Mosca, and a long succession of sociologists to this day. Essentially nonbureaucratic motivations and actions are surely necessary in actual life to keep in motion the operations of bureaucracies. Even so, Weber's portrait of the bureaucrat comes sufficiently close to produce the shock of recognition, to give this portrait much of the same kind of acceptance by large, and in our day increasingly hostile, numbers of the public and the same kind of power in human consciousness that Marx's portraits of capitalist and worker have proved to have. When G. K. Chesterton once described the bureaucrat as "an inverted Micawber, always waiting for something to turn down," he could have been speaking for Weber, at least in his final years, and for a long line of Weber's successors who have also painted the bureaucrat in these sociological tones. Chesterton could also have been speaking for many millions of Western Europeans for whom modern democracy had become increasingly a thicket of offices, agencies, and bureaus containing bureaucrats, cold, impersonal, aloof, rule-bound, and tyrannical, utterly wanting in the habits of the heart.

THE INTELLECTUAL

Among the several role-types thrown upon the landscape by currents of history in the late eighteenth and early nineteenth centuries, none has proven more important in contemporary society than that of the intellectual. I refer to those individuals who quite literally live by their wits or by the resources of their knowledge about some aspect, small or large, of the world, society, or man. Added to this is a certain adversary status with respect to culture and the social order, a built-in polemical, critical, even combative stance with respect to the norms and dogmas by which most of us live. Literary in mode of expression, given to the writing of essays, reviews, and books for the most part, the intellectual is, despite a by-now familiar posture of alienation from society, very much an element among the controlling forces in modern society, not only Western but non-Western as well in the present century.

Men of knowledge have always existed; certainly since the first great civilizations made their appearance in Asia and in the Mediterranean setting several thousand years ago. But until approximately the eighteenth century it was rare for any man of knowledge to be unconnected with some major institution in the social order—with church and state preeminently, but with other institutions as well from time to time. The unattached, loose, or freelance intellectual was a rare being, as was indeed the artist. During the Middle Ages, the West was rife with those men of knowledge whom today we would call intellectuals, but they were overwhelmingly attached, and very closely, to the church, to the university, the monastery, and, in the later phases of medieval culture, to the emerging national state. In medieval society the man of knowledge was no more distinct as such than any one of literally dozens of craftsmen or workers. Intellectuals were organized into guilds just as were fullers, apothecaries, beggars, and stonemasons.

The *philosophes* of the French Enlightenment were probably the first, in any significant number, of the modern genus of intellectual, considered, that is, as a class. Prescient as Burke so often was, he is among the first, if not the very first, to identify this new class, which he referred to as "political men of letters." It was the mark of this class, as Burke realized, that lack of firm connection with any major institution was its starting-point in its works. Hostile to the church, indeed to almost every form of religion, contemptuous of aristocracy (though never averse to accepting fees and other payments when they were available), critical of all existing forms of goverment—though not of the absolute power that resided in political sovereignty—rarely if ever to be found in any regular salaried position which might give them roots in the social order, the *philosophes* in late-eighteenth-century France really created the mold for what has proved to be an unending line of individuals forming a role-type whose essence was intellect united with an adversary position toward the mores of society.

Burke thought that the "political men of letters" in France, among whom he placed such powerful minds as Rousseau, Voltaire, and the Encyclopedists, were in large degree responsible for the French Revolution as the result of their liaisons with the new class of financial speculators and with strategically placed governmental figures, and of what Burke regarded as their generally inflammatory effect upon the middle class and even certain militant elements of the lower classes. This is not the place to assess the correctness of Burke's ascription of influence to the *philosophes* in the Revolution. I am concerned only with the fact that in his *Reflections* he commenced, as it were, the portrait of the modern political intellectual, one to which the hands of a continuing succession of portraitists have been applied.

Auguste Comte too had an early appreciation of the new class of intellectuals that had made its appearance before the Revolution and been greatly expanded in influence through this event. Comte,

in his *Positive Philosophy*, published in the 1830s, refers "to the class
which is essentially one under two names—the civil lawyers and
the metaphysicians, or, under their common title, the lawyers and
men of letters." So bad have things become, Comte continues, that
genuinely learned and wise individuals have been superseded "by
mere men of letters, so that now, any man who can hold a pen may
aspire to the spiritual regulation of society, through press or from
the professional chair, unconditionally, whatever may be his quali-
fication." The course of history, Comte believed, was from the
religious-organic, through the "critical" or "metaphysical" stage, to
the final redemptive "Positive" stage in which man would at last
find true freedom and security. No one who has read Comte carefully can doubt that it is the second, the intermediate, stage that
arouses his greatest hatred, even though he declares it crucial in the
historical sense so far as termination of the obsolete religious phase
of mankind is concerned, thus making possible the creation of a
new, Positivist organic order. The rootless, unattached intellectual,
the political man of letters, will not, however, Comte emphasizes,
have any place whatever in the great new order, founded basically
upon the religion of science, that Comte and his disciples dreamed
of.

It is, though, Tocqueville to whom we looked for the earliest distinct portrait of the intellectual in modern society. His treatment,
in *The Old Regime and the French Revolution* published in 1856, is
masterly, and little has been added in substance, I would argue, by
the succession of those such as Durkheim, Weber, and Mannheim
who have subsequently tried their hand at this subject. Tocqueville
recognized clearly that the very commitment to rational values,
above all others, on the part of the intellectual made for unending
warfare between the intellectual and the "ridiculous, ramshackle institutions, survivals of an earlier age, which no one had attempted
to coordinate or to adjust to modern conditions. . . ." Given the
conglomerate of institutions and customs which have descended
willy-nilly from the past, it "was natural enough that thinkers of
the day should come to loathe everything that savored of the past

and should desire to remold society on entirely new lines, traced by each thinker in the light of reason."

Not that Tocqueville was an admirer, either by temperament or intellectual thrust, of the political intellectuals of his own day or of the pre-Revolutionary period. And he is distinctly hostile to what he sees as the impact of the intellectual upon the course of government. In his *Recollections*, written in 1850 and 1851 to describe the events of 1848 in France and his own participation in them, Tocqueville is frequently critical of the passion for grand causes and systems he finds in the intellectual mind. His contrast of politicians and intellectuals is arresting:

I have come across men of letters, who have written history without taking part in public affairs, and politicians who have only concerned themselves with producing events without thinking of describing them. I have observed that the first are always inclined to find general causes, whereas the others, living in the midst of disconnected daily facts, are prone to imagine that everything is attributable to particular incidents and that the wires which they pull are the same that move the world. It is to be presumed that both are equally deceived.

For my part I detest these absolute systems, which represent all the events of history as depending upon great first causes linked by the chain of fatality, and which, as it were, suppress men from the history of the human race. They seem narrow, to my mind, under their pretence of broadness, and false beneath their air of mathematical exactness. . . .

There is a certain irony, even humor, in Tocqueville's characterization of the intellectual. He was himself an intellectual, and one capable, moreover, of precisely the kind of broad generalization, utilization of ideas of necessity, and recourse to the abstract that he condemns in the passage just quoted. He was to be sure a mind of genius, but he was never lacking in those qualities of the intellectual he so skillfully portrayed in all of his writings.

In history, philosophy, sociology, and literature alike, the intellectual's diversely constituted portrait is to be found in the nineteenth century. It is then that the role of the intellectual becomes not only securely fixed but also the subject of consideration ranging from the adulatory to the hostile, from the solemn to the ironic and satiric. Early in the century, in some of Thomas Love Peacock's novels (forerunners to those with which Aldous Huxley would begin his career in our own age), particularly in *Nightmare Abbey* and *Headlong Hall*, we find the Romantic intellectual portrayed, with values and ideals resplendent and rhetorical ambiguity at every turn, in accents of irony. So do intellectuals walk through the pages of Disraeli's novels, and Dickens can be found caricaturing them in several places, not least in the final pages of *David Copperfield*. H. G. Wells, in this century, after he turned from his early interest in science fantasy to the realistic novels of his middle period, gave rather more serious regard to portrayal of the intellectual, perhaps most notably in *Mr. Britling Sees It Through*. E. M. Forster, in *Howards End*, personified the intellectual in each of the Schlegel sisters. What the late Lionel Trilling wrote on this novel in his study of Forster is telling:

> . . . [O]ne of the complications of the intellectual's life is his relation to people who are not intellectuals. The very fact of being articulate, of making articulateness a preoccupation, sets up a barrier between the intellectual and the non-intellectual. The intellectual, the "freest" of men, consciously the most liberated from class, is actually the most class-marked and class-bound of all men. . . . The relation of the intellectual to the lower classes is no less confused. There is a whole mass of mankind, the enormous majority, indeed, whom he considers it his duty to "protect." To these people he vaguely supposes himself to be in a benevolent superior relation, paternal, pedagogic, even priestlike.

There are passages in Mark, Durkheim, above all in Weber and Simmel, which provide solid sociological footing for Trilling's characterization of Forster's novel and its characters. Marx (himself, of course, an intellectual of the first water) could wax scornful indeed of those writers and thinkers who, imagining themselves objective contemplators of the scene around them, were in truth, as Marx did not hesitate to declare, but hirelings and lackeys of the economic masters they served, whether consciously or unconsciously. To be sure, there is room for redemption in the intellectual's life and relation to history. After all, it is to the intellectual that Marx, and after him the Marxists, looked for formation of the vanguard that could alone mobilize the proletariat in battle for its own interests: the Communist intellectual, the intellectual who, having been made aware of the real nature of economic society and thus in a sense liberated from his historic root in this society, could become at once the prophet and the militant leader of those forces struggling for recognition in history.

Both Weber and Simmel were fascinated by the role of the intellectual not only in their own age but historically as well. Neither could muster up much optimism for the fate of the intellectual in the future. Weber thought that the processes of rationalization which had enveloped so many other spheres of society would in time include the intellectual also, reducing the pursuit of ideas to the same kind of mechanical order and bureaucratic fixity that could be seen in politics, education, and religion. Simmel saw "objectification" of Western society—that is, the replacement of the personal and intimate by structures and principles increasingly external and objective—as the nemesis of the intellectual, who had, as Simmel saw it, done so much to bring about this very objectification of life, through science and technology, and through the politicization of so many of the smaller areas of life.

Two other aspects need stressing here: the quality of alienation on the one hand and of the spirit of assault on the other. From the very beginning of the post-Revolutionary Romantic movement in letters and art in Europe, the conception of the individual artist or writer, the intellectual, as somehow estranged from society and even from himself was fairly common. The intellectual, especially in the role of poet, novelist, or painter, was conceived (not least by himself) as preoccupied by beauty, truth, nobility, as being above the kinds of material considerations which drove the rest of the population. Between intellectual and social order there thus existed—had to exist, so to speak, by portrait-definition—a gulf that nothing could bridge. In the Middle Ages the intellectual—scholar, priest, artist—was considered as much a part of society as any other craftsman. In some degree, allowing only for the exception provided by the humanists in the Italian fifteenth century, this sense continued through later centuries. It is really only with the rise of the Romantic artist and writer in the late eighteenth and early nineteenth centuries that the portrait of the intellectual, as we find this in sociological and other writing, becomes increasingly tinctured by alienation and the marks of withdrawal from ordinary society.

Something else, however, is to be seen in the sociological portrait of the intellectual: power. Or rather obsession with the uses of power as applied in behalf of rational, humanitarian, and revolutionary projects. From Comte through Tocqueville to Michels and Weber this quality of the modern intellectual is given foremost place. Coupled with fascination with power is to be seen also what Lionel Trilling, in a now-famous phrase, referred to as "adversary spirit." Again we are struck by how modern this spirit is in the intellectual; as modern as the sense of alienation. For the most part, prior to the late eighteenth century, the intellectual, whether in service to church, state, or aristocratic patron, rarely if ever manifested a spirit of assault upon the verities of the establishment. It was, without doubt, the union of intellectuals and politicians in the French Revolution, and the profound sense of achievement that was created in so many minds by this union, that brought into being the power-bemused intellectual—and his portrait by sociologists in the nineteenth century.

Hence the picture of the intellectual that has reached our own age: a being motivated and governed by abstract principles for the most part, dedicated to the pursuits of the mind, often a disturber of the intellectual peace and a rebel against established verities, commonly oriented toward the intellectually and morally ideal rather than toward existing realities of interest, usually liberal-to-radical in ideology, fascinated by the humanitarian uses of power, especially central power, and, as I have emphasized, generally convinced of the existence of a wall between himself and society at large.

This is, I believe, a fair description of a role-type created in ever-enlarging numbers by the tides of industrialism and democracy; a role-type that has had manifest fascination for the sociologist since Comte and Tocqueville. In every respect the intellectual's portrait belongs with those of the bourgeois, the worker, and the bureaucrat in modern sociology, as in so many other spheres of humanistic thought.

5

The Problem of Motion

The artist's problem, writes Etienne Gilson in *Painting and Reality*, "is to obtain from the solid and immobile objects produced by his art in expression of movement, of becoming, and, in short, life."

That, basically, is the sociologist's problem too: to obtain from such structures and types as he feels obliged to construct for analytical or conceptual purposes "an expression of movement, of becoming, and, in short, life." Few things mattered as much to the sociologists of the nineteenth century as, in Comte's phrasing, the uniting of statics and dynamics; that is, the achievement, through one systematic set of principles, of an explanation of structure or order on the one hand and of change or development on the other. No matter what the structure under consideration—mankind, society, culture as a whole, or a more limited one such as capitalism, democracy, or nationalism—the overriding aim was that of obtaining movement conceived as development, what Marx called "laws of motion."

Not only sociology but nearly all other intellectual areas in the nineteenth century were fascinated by the whole idea of movement. We see it in a great deal of the philosophy of the age—Hegel's perhaps foremost. It is no less apparent in painting and sculpture where, before the century was out, a large variety of techniques for depicting movement were in use. Earlier ideals of repose and of classic formalism—signalized in landscapes, portraits, even in the uncommonly stylized battle scenes, and, wherever there was wealth and social position, in architecture and formal gardens—were succeeded in rising volume by ideals which made movement the sovereign end. Even before the Impressionists came on the scene the new appetite for motion had become evident, and by the end of the century painters and sculptors were engaged in endless effort to capture flux, motion, and energy.

Nor was literature unaffected. We know how keenly interested novelists and poets as well as essayists and critics were by the whole philosophy of evolution or development. Tennyson's "Let the great world spin forever down the ringing grooves of change" is a fitting epitaph for the author of *Locksley Hall*, a work that tells us as well as any possibly could of the attraction which lay in the ideas of progress and development. Across the Channel Victor Hugo was no less entranced by the thought of the perfection which lay ahead, the result of inexorable development. But it was not simply the content of novels and poems and plays that manifested interest in movement. Even the form or structure of literature began to be affected, with techniques sought through which movement could be more faithfully rendered. Time conceived as flow, as river, as stream, even as torrent, becomes more and more the object of the poet's or novelist's concern. To bring time, event, and structure somehow into harmony was for many creative writers, especially by the end of the century, as much of a goal as it was for sociologists and biologists.

Nor, when we are dealing with the relation of art and movement, can we forget the historians of the period. Granted that this was the century in which, especially in Germany, the ideal of a scientific history arose: that is, history from which the purely polemical and tendentious had been expunged in favor of describing the past *wie es eigentlich gewesenist*, in Ranke's celebrated phrase—that is, exactly as it happened. Granted all of this and with it the feverish exploration of archives and libraries as the means of ever-closer approximation of who said or did what exactly when, we cannot overlook the triumph in the century of history-writing as conscious Romantic art. The greatest names of the century—Bancroft, Parkman, and Motley in the United States, Macaulay, Trevelyan, Green in England, Michelet and Renan in France, and Ranke, Mommsen, and Treitschke in Germany—were one and all seeking, in consciously artistic fashion, to unite past and present in forms and techniques which borrowed heavily from the literature of the time.

In sum, the artist's search in the century for forms in which to give expression to movement, to banish the fixed and inert, is strikingly akin to the sociologist's passion for the dynamic—manifest chiefly in the perspective of evolution or development that so dominates the nineteenth century.

PANORAMA AND THE ILLUSION OF MOTION

In sociology, whether nineteenth-century or contemporary, no effort to represent movement in time is more imposing than that which we call "grand evolution." This is actually an intellectual device through which a pattern of alleged change, a sequence of asserted stages, is made central to an entity variously called Mankind, Society, or Culture. I can think of no better way of illustrating what is involved here than to draw briefly from a contemporary "grand evolutionist," Talcott Parsons. I have specific reference to his widely lauded and influential *Societies: Evolutionary and Comparative Perspectives.* The book is steeped in the basic premises and perspectives of nineteenth-century panoramic evolution. The aim of the book is to describe what Parsons calls the evolution, through variation and differentiation from simple to progressively more complex forms, of *total society* (the italics are Parsons'). In terms of what it claims to do, then, the book is of a piece with evolutionary theory in biology and other areas of modern exploration of nature. Its purported subject is *change in time.*

Actually, however, what we are given by Parsons is not in fact change or movement in time but the *illusion of movement.* The following illustration is sufficient. He is describing what he calls the evolution of marriage structure. We are first given an account of the system which prevails among the Australian aborigines, one that Parsons declares, though without supporting evidence, to be inherently unstable, one in which "we would expect structural change to become evident." Further, according to Parsons, "a potential for evolutionary advance" exists in this system, though again no evidence is adduced that really explains such a potential. Nevertheless, still following Parsons' account, we turn to the "change," the "evolutionary development" that emerges from the Australian system. Where do we find this alleged change or development or evolution? Not, most certainly, in the actual history of the Australians. For proof of his theory of evolutionary change, Parsons turns to a people many thousands of miles removed from Australia, the Shilluk of the Upper Nile in Sudan. Here, according to Parsons, a "higher stage" of marriage system is to be found, evidencing what Parsons chooses to call a "developmental breakthrough."

Now *an actual change* is a change in a persisting entity, or, as change has been well defined, *a succession of differences in time, in a persisting identity.* Thus a human being "changes" as he advances from infancy to adulthood; the United States as a nation has clearly "changed" during its first two centuries; the New York Public Library has "changed" in a score of ways since its inception; and so on. But a mere array of differences is not change. To lay out in a museum case, for instance, a collection of weapons, ranged in some predetermined order, is not to produce change: only an array of different things. But, and this is the crux, the *illusion* of change can without question be created by such an array of weapons.

The artist, writes Herbert Read in *The Art of Sculpture*, gives us "the illusion of movement. He can create this illusion in two ways only. One, which is common to painting and sculpture, is to compose in rhythmical and usually linear sequences so that the eye, following the sequential forms, so stimulates the mind that an hallucinatory sensation of movement is set up." Read's second way need not occupy us; the first is entirely sufficient here.

Now that is, of course, precisely what Talcott Parsons has done in the instance described above. A marriage form in a single culture is described and declared to be unstable, to be inherently susceptible to evolutionary change in time, and to be replaced, as it were, by another form. But for proper evidence of this evolutionary change, of any kind of change whatever, we should of course be obliged to stay with the single culture, to observe in it whatever change in fact takes place. However what Parsons provides us with is not a change at all but a different marriage form in a culture halfway across the earth from the first; yet he declares *this* to be a "change" in the form of marriage described in the original culture. It would be hard to find a better demonstration of what Read calls "the illusion of movement."

What we have, then, is not the biological scientist's evolution, based upon scientific evidence and direct observation of genetic processes of change—real change—but, instead, the attempt, in Herbert Read's words, "to compose in rhythmical and usually linear sequences" a *panorama*. That is in substance all that Parsons' work can claim to be: a vast panorama, exhibiting innumerable types and forms, all laid out or arranged in the light of some predetermined conception of artistic symmetry.

It was, however, in the nineteenth century that this form of panoramic art flourished most vividly among sociologists, anthropologists, and others in the social sciences. It is in the writings of Auguste Comte, Herbert Spencer, Lewis Morgan, and so many others of lesser note that we can best see the panoramas which in that century were placed under the rubric of grand or systematic evolution. It is of some interest, and leads to further development of my point in this section, to see the background of the rise in the nineteenth century of this intrinsically artistic, that is, panoramic, venture. A brief excursion into the history of ideas is important here.

For nearly three millennia philosophers in the West had been preoccupied by what Aristotle called the *scala naturae*, the scale, or hierarchy, of nature, revealed in the *logical* progression of entities in nature from the simplest to the most complex. This is what the late

A. O. Lovejoy referred to in a book of that title as *the great chain of being*. Note that what Lovejoy means by "the chain of being" is the unbroken hierarchy of living forms that philosophers perceived, or imagined to exist, all the way from the smallest and simplest of organisms on earth up to God. Life, it was declared—by philosophers from Plato and Aristotle through the Romans and the Christian philosophers of the Middle Ages to the eighteenth-century *philosophes* and their contemporaries—may be conceived as forming a continuous chain of being, a ladder, if we like, that is without break in continuity. Not only organisms but also peoples and cultures, as philosophers long before the modern age asserted, may be so arranged conceptually, so set forth for the mind's contemplation.

Until the eighteenth century, however, as Lovejoy points out, this chain of being was regarded as almost wholly a static, a purely classificatory, series of entities. There was only rarely a glimpse of the possibility that the chain of being might also be envisaged as something dynamic, as a record of the actual development or evolution that life, and also society, have undergone over a very long period of time.

Even in the eighteenth century, although ideas of evolution, both biological and social, were widely present, as many historians of the subject have described, it was rare for the dynamic possibility inherent in the chain of being to be brought out explicitly. For throughout the centuries the emphasis in nearly all treatments of this conceptual chain had been on its timelessness, its eternality. "A world of time and change," writes Lovejoy, "is a world which can neither be deduced from nor reconciled with the postulate that existence is the expression and consequence of a sytem of 'eternal' ar 'necessary' truths inherent in the very logic of being." It was, for the most part, sufficient, in other words, to show, or to argue, the scalar continuity of being—either by way of demonstrating God's provision for "plenitude" or simply to show, as Aristotle and his successors had, the intrinsic "plenitude" of nature: plenitude and also hierarchical character.

It was, so far as we know, Turgot, in 1750, who first showed

awareness of the possibility of instilling in the chain of being, at
least so far as the logical hierarchy of cultures and peoples on earth
was concerned, a principle of motion or movement. Turgot, in a
now-famous discourse delivered at the Sorbonne in the latter part
of 1750, saw this chain as one exemplifying, giving witness to, the
actual development through time of mankind, or as Turgot put it,
the human mind.

All ages are linked together by a chain of causes and effects which unite
the present state of the world with everything that has preceded it. . . .
The inequality of nations increases [with development through time]; here
the arts start to develop; there they advance with long steps toward perfection. In one place they are arrested in their mediocrity; in another the
primal darkness is not yet wholly dispelled; and through these infinitely
varied inequalities, the present state of the world, in presenting *every shade*
of barbarism and civilization, gives us at a single glance all the monuments,
the vestiges, *of each step taken by the human mind,* the likeness of each stage it
has passed through, the history of the ages [italics added].

Now, innocuous though that passage must be for anyone in our
day acquainted with even the rudiments of the theory of social and
cultural evolution, it must be accounted one of the major
breakthroughs of the eighteenth century in the study of society.
Not, really, until the next century, in the works of the sociologists
I am about to mention, are all the implications of Turgot's statement realized, but no one can take away from Turgot credit for
converting into dynamic terms a conceptual series—that is, the
chain of being—that had for so long been represented statically.
Others in the eighteenth century, such as Montesquieu, had looked
out on all the social and cultural differences in the world and had
accounted, or tried to account, for them in climatic, topographical,
or racial terms. It was left for Turgot to see these differences as
being exemplifications, "monuments," as he put it, of an actual
order of development, a progressive order, taken by the human
mind over countless millennia. Merely to look at the very simple,
the rudest, of cultures today, is to see exactly what the beginnings
of Western civilization were in the very distant past. Again we see
what can only be called the illusion of change. An array of dif-

ferences, to repeat, is not in itself a change: merely an array of differences. But if this array of peoples and cultures is appropriately arranged, and if to the array there is added the intuitive vision of some powerful, if unprovable, unverifiable, *vis genetrix,* some principle of constant, continuous, *development,* then the illusion of motion is made complete. Just as complete as is the sense of motion we get from one or other of the magnificent representations of battle or war in mural or tapestry—the famous Bayeux tapestry chronicling the Norman Conquest will serve nicely here—which we find in the world's museums.

Panorama: the illusion of movement: this is what we are actually given in the notable works of the nineteenth-century grand evolutionists. Herbert Spencer, always candid, has given us, in his *Autobiography,* an explicit account of how he put together his massive *Principles of Sociology* in which, according to the stated purpose of the book, the origin and development of each of the major institutions in society are dealt with and explained. Kinship, class, economy, religion, government—all of these and others are dealt with by Spencer under the claimed theory of development or evolution. The book is filled with illustrations, thousands of them, of Spencer's theory of mankind's development. Now how did Spencer reach all of this? As I say, he is perfectly candid. All his life, he tells us, he kept small file cards or slips; on each was written a brief account of some cultural trait as found in a given people. Thousands, even tens of thousands, of these cards were made by Spencer and then filed in drawers arranged logically in accord with Spencer's already formed idea of what the course of mankind's evolution in each and every institution had been. When it came time actually to write the book, Spencer explains, it was simply a matter of taking out cards one by one and converting their contents into the text of his vast *Principles.* We may say it was a taxonomist's way of proceeding; but it was also, in the strict sense, the artist's: through adroit use of pattern, of design, the illusion of movement is created in the reader's mind. All that is provided us is an immense range of traits, just as if they were laid out in some mammoth museum case; traits ranging from, say, animism or totemism in religion all the way to the Christian Eucharist or Muslim sacrifice. But, given the claimed existence of progressive evolution in time, arrived at, as we know, intuitively, and given too the sheer symmetry of the array of instances, we are persuaded into believing that what we are actually reading is an account of movement in time. But it is not movement; only the illusion of movement, just as we get this in an Impressionist painting of a square in Paris or in something like the Victory of Samothrace where the artful design of the marble makes us believe the goddess's garments really are flying in the wind.

It is the same with Comte's notable and extremely influential *Positive Philosophy*, published in the 1830s. Comte is concerned with the progressive development of knowledge throughout the life of mankind. This development moves, he tells us, through the three stages of the "religious," the "metaphysical," and the "positive" or scientific. Again what we are given in actual substance is nothing more than an array, an artfully contrived series of peoples in time and space. "From the wretched inhabitants of Tierra del Fuego to the most advanced nations of Western Europe, there is no social grade which is not extant in some points of the globe, and usually in localities which are clearly apart." Eighty years earlier Turgot had made the same point in almost identical language.

The anthropologist E. B. Tylor, in his seminal writings on culture, made the same point, created the same visual panorama, the same illusion of movement: "[T]he institutions of man are as distinctly stratified as the earth on which he lives. They succeed each other in series substantially uniform over the globe, independent of what seem comparatively superficial differences of race and language, but shaped by similar human nature acting through successively changed conditions in savage, barbaric, and civilized life."

The American Lewis H. Morgan, in *Ancient Society*, a work that exerted great influence upon Marx and Engels, carried the whole panoramic idea to its logical completion. In this book, largely concerned with the three great institutions of government, kinship, and property, we find a vast array of peoples presented in carefully contrived fashion. Some are living peoples such as the Iroquois, the Hawaiians, and the Highland Scots; some are ancient in the Western world, such as the Greeks, the Romans, and the Germanic invaders; still others, such as the Aztecs, fall in a separate class. What Morgan does, however, is take all of these peoples, present and past, and arrange them in such a way as to demonstrate panoramically "the evolution" of human society, that is, the movement of "man" through long vistas of time. We find American Indians, Aztecs, early Greeks, and Romans placed side by side, in immediate sequence, despite the enormous distances of time and place, in order to demonstrate Morgan's theory of movement in time. But it is all, of course, "the illusion of movement," the kind of illusion that only panorama can provide through use of techniques of linear sequence best known to the artist.

What Spencer wrote in 1857, two years before publication by Darwin of his classic, served to express the obsession of movement conceived as development of a large number of minds: "Whether it be in the development of the Earth, in the development of life upon its surface, in the development of Society, of Government, of Manufactures, of Commerce, of Language, Literature, Science, Art, this same evolution of the simple into the complex, through successive differentiations, holds throughout." Earlier Hegel, in his *Philosophy of History*, had written: "The principle of development involves also the existence of a latent germ of being—a capacity or potentiality striving to realize itself. This formal conception finds actual existence in spirit; which has the history of the world for its theatre. . . . Development, however, is also a property of organized natural objects."

Development, in short, was omnipresent as an idea or theme in nineteenth-century thought. The great Christian theologian John Henry Newman, who was to become a cardinal in the Roman Catholic Church after his momentous conversion from the Anglican faith, wrote, in 1845, a book with the title *Development of Christian Doctrine*. The expressed purpose of Newman's work was to

show that the difference between the Christianity of his own day
and that of the apostolic beginnings of the religion was one simply
of development, of the simple becoming the complex, the homogeneous the heterogeneous. And this, be it noted, years before Darwin published his *Origin of Species* or Spencer *The Development Hypothesis*. In point of fact, a whole succession of works in biology (we
need start no earlier than those of Charles Darwin's grandfather,
Erasmus, in the late eighteenth century) sought to demonstrate the
genetic descent of the species from one another. It is interesting to
note in any treatment of the unity of science and art that Erasmus
Darwin chose verse as the means of setting forth observations and
theories concerning the ecological relationships of the organic
world and also the evolutionary process contained from the very
beginning in this world.

No mistake in the history of ideas could be greater, in sum, than
that of supposing Charles Darwin's *Origin of Species,* published in
1859, to be the single source of the idea of development. In scores
of contexts, philosophical, artistic, and other, we find the spirit of
developmentalism, of measured, ordered movement through time,
a dominant one in the whole of the nineteenth century, indeed in
the final decades of the preceding century. Such an observation is
designed in no way to detract from the spectacular influence of
Darwin's work. How influential it was, and also how well prepared
the ground was for its acceptance, can be inferred from the near-
dozen editions the *Origin of Species* went through within a decade or
so after initial publication. Granted there are insights and observations peculiar to Darwin's work alone, or shared at most with
Wallace and one or two other biologists: the fact remains that the
instant appeal of the work depended on the prevalence of the whole
panoramic envisagement of movement in time in so many areas of
thought in the age. Nor was Darwin a stranger to the use of panorama: the arranging of flora and fauna observed in many parts of
the world into genera and species and other forms or types. The
enormous emphasis that Darwin places on what he calls "the geo-
logic record," that is, the geological strata, each with its preserved

fossiliferous specimens, is not different in its way from the "strata" of extant peoples which were used by Comte, Spencer, Morgan, and others. Without the artist's vision of panorama, in short, it is doubtful whether the idea of universal movement in time would ever have assumed the place it did in both philosophy and science.

DIORAMA

We have been concerned with large-scale, grand, or what I have called panoramic envisagement of asserted movement in time, involving such entities as Mankind, Society, or Culture, each abstract and universal in character. I want now to turn to a different, although closely related, treatment of movement that is manifest in nineteenth-century sociological thought. For this the word *diorama* seems appropriate. Diorama, the dictionary tells us, is "a scene, commonly in miniature, reproduced in three dimensions by placing objects, figures, etc. in front of a painted background." The hand of the artist, as well as the artist's intuitive, iconic vision, is no less important here than it is in the panoramic representation of development. But the immediate featured entity and scene are smaller. It may be, as with Marx, capitalism; or as with Tocqueville, equality; or as with Weber, what he called rationalization. Each is dealt with, however, in the light of a larger background of historical reality conceived in terms of some master-theme.

Again it is useful to cite the passage with which I began this chapter: The artist's problem, Gilson tells us, "is to obtain from the solid and immobile objects produced by his art an expression of movement, of becoming, and, in short, life." What we find, alongside panoramic envisagements of reality, are constructs of the sociological mind smaller in size, more highly structured, in which the object remains that of deriving principles of motion or development in time. To create the impression of ordered development, of *becoming,* through the rendering of the details of structure is just as much the nineteenth-century sociologist's way of working as it is the artist's. Marx's *Capital* is a diorama, complete with figures called workers and capitalists and with constructs called factories and offices; and out of this diorama comes the sense of movement, of becoming, for the reader just as surely as the same sense is given to us by the sculptor working with a block of marble or the painter with brushes and oils on canvas. The same is true of Tocqueville's *Democracy in America*, also a diorama, constructed in approximately the same period in which Marx constructed his equally memorable one. But what Tocqueville gives us, by contrast, are figures known as citizens, politicians, and bureaucrats, and structures called democracy, equality, and centralized power. He too leaves the reader with the deep feeling not simply of form and content but of motion, of ordered development in time. So, finally, is Weber's classic treatment of bureaucracy in modern life a diorama, with figures and structures drawn, as it were, from both Marx and Tocqueville.

Now, behind each of these dioramas, it is important to stress, is to be seen a large backdrop, so to speak, that is a philosophy of history covering many centuries. Marx gives us a panoramic movement of society that he identifies in several places as proceeding from ancient slavery through feudalism to capitalism and, eventually, to socialism. We cannot really understand the kind of thinking that went into Marx's *Capital* without seeing the book as a "constructed image," to use Herbert Read's phrase, against a background on which the whole of human history has been painted. As I noted above, both Marx and Engels were deeply impressed by Lewis Morgan's *Ancient Society*, as indeed they were by Darwin's *Origin of Species*, and it is fair to say that the panorama presented by a Lewis Morgan lies indispensably behind the diorama that is Marx's *Capital*.

My concern, though, is entirely with Marx's rendering of capitalism, the structure he generated conceptually as the means of giving symmetry, harmony, and also movement to the otherwise chaotic scene around him. What we are given in the Marxian diorama is a scene composed of exploited workers, exploiting capitalists, the fetishism of commodities, value created only by labor with an inevitable surplus value which is the result of the workers' inability to buy back what they produce, ineluctable growth of the proletariat and of concentration of capital, and, giving dynamism to the whole setting, an ineradicable conflict between the two great classes, workers and capitalists.

This is, of course, the essence of *Capital*, Marx's greatest work. There were many economists in the nineteenth century for whom equilibrium or balance was the essence of the capitalist system. Many thought that profits, rent, wages, and interest all coexisted in relative harmony. The constant drive in the capitalist system was thus toward equilibrium. Not so for Marx! What he saw, with artist's eye, as he looked out on the infinitely diverse assemblage of shops, offices, factories, mills, farms, and estates of his day is one thing alone: incessant, unquenchable conflict between two great encapsulating classes, the bourgeoisie and the proletariat, a conflict that arises directly, Marx argued, from the very nature of profit resting on private ownership of the means of production. Under the profit system, it is impossible for the working class to receive more than a subsistence wage; competition for jobs within this class ensures that. Thus with the profit system there is "surplus value," the surplus left in goods produced which subsistence wages are incapable of purchasing. Hence, Marx concludes, there is in capitalism a built-in tendency toward contradiction and conflict. The contradictions bred by private property and profit accumulate, capital becomes steadily more concentrated, the proletarianization of the social order proceeds relentlessly, and the necessary consequence of all this structurally built-in dynamism is revolution in the most highly developed industrial countries; revolution that will be followed by dictatorship of the proletariat and then classless society, socialism.

Such perceptions are as vivid as any to be found in nineteenth-century literature and art. That Marx's specific predictions have not been fulfilled, that his analysis of the capitalist economy has been widely pronounced defective, that his depiction of contradictions and other processes of movement in the economic structure is no more verifiable than, say, a novel by Zola or a sketch by

Daumier, none of these considerations really affect the matter. The Marxian vision is without question one of the three or four most powerful and encompassing world-visions to be found in the twentieth century; only Christianity and Islam give it serious rivalry. But with all allowance made for Marx's erudition and his historic impact upon the social sciences, especially sociology, it is as art united with prophecy, virtually religious prophecy, that Marxism survives. He was one of those in the century who saw action, dynamism, and unfolding movement in structures and processes which others regarded as static.

There is nothing strange in the fact that Marx as a youth was a full Romantic in almost every sense of the word. It is only too evident that behind his early poems burned the soul of not only the Romantic artist but the romantic revolutionist or nihilist. Later years would transform the tools with which Marx worked—from those of the artist proper to those of the philosopher and, as Marx believed, scientist. But no one reading *Capital* can doubt that, for all the intimidating apparatus of concept and principle, the artistic spirit lives.

Let us turn now to another masterful rendering of motion in nineteenth-century social thought. This is Tocqueville's, particularly as it is to be seen in his own great diorama, *Democracy in America*. Despite the title, the book is, as many reviewers even at the time of publication emphasized, more concerned with Western Europe than with America. It is precisely the same Europe that fascinated Marx and elicted from him *Capital*. But how very different are Tocqueville's arrangement of figures and structures and the principle of motion he extracts from them. Not the economic but the political is dominant in Tocqueville's setting, not capitalists and workers so much as voters, citizens, and bureaucrats.

The Paris Tocqueville had grown up in was without question one of the most seminal contexts of the creative mind Western society has yet given us. Goethe regarded Paris in this light, and there were others on both sides of the Atlantic to share his views. Writers, painters, sculptors, scientists, journalists of extraordinary excellence populated the city. It was at one and the same time the intellectual center of political conservatism and of radicalism. At one extreme, such conservatives as Maistre, Bonald, and the young Lamennais (who was later to join in first liberal, then radical movements) wrote in behalf of monarchy, aristocracy, and ultramontane Catholicism. At the other extreme were radicals like Proudhon, Blanc, Cabet, and, not to be overlooked, Marx himself, whose few years in Paris in the early 1840s had, as we know, decisive influence on his mind. In between the extremes lay numerous degrees and kinds of political and social sensitivity, reflected as often in the short stories and novels of the age as in the tracts and tomes of the militant.

Tocqueville will always be most famous, no doubt, for *Democracy in America,* and that work is without question a classic in Americana, unrivaled as an interpretation of the United States until, a full generation later, Bryce wrote *The American Commonwealth.* But, as Tocqueville himself tells us in the Introduction to the first part of that work, published in 1835, it was not so much America that he and his companion Beaumont had gone to see as "the image of democracy." And when the full work was completed, with Part II appearing in 1840, it was only too evident that Tocqueville all along had been much more interested in creating an ideal-type of democracy from which he could derive impressions analytical and prophetic than he was in ethnographic description of the lives of the Americans. We know from his letters that he had pretty well composed the book, in outline and thrust at least, before he visited the United States, in which he remained for less than a year, and that this outline and thrust had been largely germinated by Tocqueville's precocious speculations on the toll that was being exacted in the West by egalitarianism.

Given the Paris in which Tocqueville came of age, it is hardly surprising that equality would become for him not only the central value of modernity but also the mainspring of social development. There were in Paris dozens of intellectuals, artists, philosophers, students, and others similarly preoccupied by equality. If the Rev-

olution at the end of the preceding century had given birth to the
ideal, there were many more forces in the nineteenth century to
keep it vital, to generate growth. It was, though, Tocqueville who
did the most to convert the concept of equality from a mere value
or condition into a powerful process of development, into something dynamic and forward-moving. And like Marx, Tocqueville
constructs his diorama of democracy against a panoramic backdrop
in which a dozen centuries are revealed.

Like Marx, Tocqueville saw the dynamic processes of the
present as lineal results of an historical tendency centuries old.
From the late Middle Ages on, Tocqueville writes in his Introduction, every major event, including the Crusades, the introduction
of gunpowder, the invention of mass-printing, the Reformation,
along with others, has facilitated the spread of equalization in society. "Running through the pages of our history, there is hardly an
important event in the last seven hundred years which has not
turned out to be advantageous for equality."

In his later, almost equally epochal work, *The Old Regime and the
French Revolution,* Tocqueville traced, from the Middle Ages on,
though with special attention to the period 1450–1750, the advancement of equality that proceeded from the incessant central-
ization of power under the monarchy and its bureaucracy, thus
leveling the aristocracy, the estates, and the historic local governments. This work, as we know, was designed as the first part of
what was to be a longer study of "the European Revolution" whose
completion was alas, prevented by Tocqueville's untimely death,
which left us with only his scattered notes. Tocqueville was, as
every major historian of the French Revolution has noted, a con-
summate historian.

It is not his role as historian, though, that is central to my dis-
cussion here. It is rather as portraitist or landscapist of the democratic society of his day that he earned a lasting place in the literature of social philosophy. I have mentioned above Tocqueville's
central place in creating the vision of the masses in European writing, and here all I want to do is stress his equal importance as artist

concerned with the rendering of movement or motion. For the essence of Tocqueville's detailing of equality—the central value of the modern Western world, in his view—is equality's inherent, uncontrollable, limitless power of expansion, of extension into all areas of man's life. Others in his day saw only a legal or political value, a more or less shapeless condition; Tocqueville, summoning up all the powers of the born artist, presented equality for what it was in fact in his mind: endless movement, development, becoming.

My last illustration of sociological diorama is Weber's treatment of rationalization, a concept or condition we have already glanced at, for it figures in landscape and portrait alike in Weber's work. For Weber too there is background for his diorama of the bureaucratic-rational scene around him. Well before Weber's life-work was completed, he had come to see the entire Western world, and much else too in the history of civilization, in a very large degree under the rubric of rationalization. Just as Marx could endow the occasional instances of class conflict he observed around him with dynamic significance that extended over the whole of human history, as Tocqueville could convert a single value, equality, into a whole principle of Western social and cultural development, so Weber, responding with like sensitivity, saw motion, movement, and unfolding in rationality, or rather in the subjection to rationalist structural processes of spheres ranging from music to politics.

Basically, rationalization is, in Weber's sense of the word, the imposition of strict means-end criteria not only upon thought itself but upon art, science, culture, government, war, even religion. It implies the exclusion from thought or act of all that is purely traditional, charismatic, or ritualistic, all, in short, that is not directly related to the means necessary to efficient realization of a given end. Since reason teaches us that the shortest distance between two points is a straight line, rationalization is the process through which we seek, as it were, a straight line, and, thereby, avoid or exclude all that is indirect or circuitous. Weber came to believe that from the late Middle Ages on, more and more areas of Western culture, beginning with government and finance, had become subject to the canons of rationalization, thus promoting what he called, in a phrase borrowed from the poet Schiller, "the disenchantment of the world." In both *Science as Vocation* and *Politics as Vocation* Weber gave eloquent emphasis to his conviction that in each area there had taken place in modern Western history a process best described as the substitution of rational, formal, and logical principles for those of sacred, traditional, and folk character.

Capitalism for Weber was best characterized not in the terms which the classical and Marxian economists had made central— profit, rent, wages, and capital itself—but, rather, in terms of conversion of what Toennies had called *Gemeinschaft* relationships to *Gesellschaft*, with the conscious effort to achieve through rational calculation of means and consequences what had been before left to use and wont, to tradition or to sacred, moral, and esthetic considerations. Capitalism, in Weber's view, arose when, as in the Europe of the fifteenth and sixteenth centuries, rational principles of accounting began to prevail, when the idea of a "rational" or "free" market of labor and of capital began to gain currency, and when, with the increasing triumph of technology, principles of division of labor and specialization took command in manufacture. From the strict point of view of production in quantity, the factory was manifestly a more "rational" means than, say, cottage industry or the putting-out system.

It was Weber's distinctive merit to see economic rationalization as the master-category within which capitalism and modern socialism alike fall. What was primary for Weber was not abstract ownership of property, that is, whether "public" or "private," but rather the means of organization of property. Weber saw an organizational revolution taking place in his time, and from his point of view socialism was but a more advanced (in the strictly logical sense) form of capitalism. The essential means-end schema affecting management and workers, technology and goods, producers and consumers, would remain, albeit in modified form, under socialism.

It is, however, in the sphere of political authority that Weber applied most fruitfully, and with more lasting effect, his theme of rationalization. Whereas in the medieval world, all authority, like all rights and liberties, had been "personal"—that is, inseparable from the individual possessing the authority—the trend of modern history has been, Weber argues, toward the transfer of authority from person to office. Bureaucracy is simply the structuring of authority in terms of impersonal positions and offices rather than specific, identifiable individuals. The ideal-type of bureaucracy is the system in which all reliance upon the traditional, the ritualistic, the charismatic, or the personal is terminated; considerations of emotion or sentiment are excluded; and values alien to efficiency of operation are abolished. Weber did not, of course, suppose that so "perfect" a system of bureaucracy ever had or ever could be brought into actual existence. He was well aware of the intrusive effects of sentiment, tradition, informal relationships, and ritual in the best-run bureaucracies. He nevertheless saw in the development of the modern West the gradual triumph, not merely in government but in industry, education, religion, the military, and other spheres of the bureaucratic, of the rationalistic.

Even in music, as he made specific in a short work on the subject, the principle of rationalization may be seen operating in the transition from the phrasings, melodic lines, and harmonic structures of medieval or early-modern Europe to those of the music of masters such as Mozart, Beethoven, and Berlioz. So too, as he points out, has the improvement of technology, extended to the technology of instrumentation of the modern symphony orchestra, represented the effect of rationalization. Even the organization of the orchestra, the increasing utilization of sections of instruments, and the increasing importance of the conductor, the arranger, and other specialists attest to the triumph of the principle of rationalization in Western society. There is, finally, not only in music but in the arts as a whole, the increasing division between artist and public, between performer and audience, that matches the division between specialist and layman, between bureaucracy and the governed, in wider areas of life.

Thus we see that for Weber, as for Comte, Marx, Tocqueville, and many another nineteenth-century sociologist, a single form of relationship, a condition, that to other eyes could seem no more than a static, intermittent, occasional aspect of the landscape, was susceptible to transformation into a dynamic principle, a law of movement. If to some eyes, in Weber's day as in ours, there is an illusory quality to rationalization conceived as a principle of historical development, precisely the same may be, and has been, said of Comte's progress, Marx's class-conflict, and Tocqueville's equality. The art element is inescapable, and we may quote from Herbert Read's *The Art of Sculpture:* "Movement, of course, takes place in time, *and is only observable as a temporal displacement of matter*" (italics added). Or, to state the matter differently, all change—and most especially the kind of change we call development or growth—is an inference we draw from essentially static materials. Only that kind of imagination that, as I have argued, in this book, is common to the artist and scientist is capable of seizing upon and describing, or otherwise expressing, motion and movement.

6
The Rust of Progress

Throughout the nineteenth century, side by side with the spirit of progress that so plainly animates the minds of the larger number of philosophers and social scientists, there is to be seen slowly but certainly developing a kind of malaise affecting the very premises on which the spirit of progress rested. It is not easy to describe succinctly this malaise; it is enough to say at this point that it is to be found in some of the most original and prophetic thinkers of the century, among them Tocqueville, Burckhardt, Nietzsche, and, as I shall indicate in some detail, sociologists of the stature of Toennies, Weber, Durkheim, and Simmel. What gives this malaise its distinctive character is that it is founded upon a reaction to precisely the same elements of modernity which figured so prominently in the major expressions of the vision of Western progress: industrialism, technology, mass democracy, egalitarianism, science, secularism, and individual liberation from traditional values. Such diverse minds as Bentham, Mill, Marx, Spencer, and Lester Ward could see, though from very different vantage points, almost limitless progress for mankind flowing from these. But the minds I am chiefly concerned with in this chapter, while by no means denying progress in some degree as the result of the elements mentioned, were more prone to see what I have chosen to call "the rust of progress"; that is, infirmities in the human condition directly caused by "progress."

The malaise I speak of reaches its climax toward the end of the nineteenth century, but, as I have noted, it is present in varying intensity throughout the century. We get intimations of it from Burke's *Reflections on the Revolution in France* published in 1790. There Burke, presciently noting the qualities in the French experience which would prove fundamental in the development of democracy in the nineteenth century, which indeed would constitute the democratic revolution, warned of what would be, he thought, nothing less than a "general earthquake" in the Western world. The combination of worship of individual freedom and the *populus*, on the one hand, and, on the other, the erosive effects upon society of the new business class and the new bureaucracy would, Burke tells us, prove destructive in the long run of all that had made Western civilization great.

Burke was far from alone. In France the young Lamennais, in his *Essay on Indifference*, said as much. Bonald, chief social philosopher of conservatism in France, constructed the rudiments of a whole sociology of power undergirded by moral chaos around the same depredations he could see being effected on traditional society. Alexis de Tocqueville, after finishing the first part of *Democracy in America* with a veritable ode to American progress, wrote the second part in a strikingly different state of mind, which led him to see long-run desuetude, even collapse, resulting from the very values and ways of behavior which were everywhere being hailed in his day. So did Burckhardt, author of the respendent study of the Italian Renaissance, come increasingly to see the future of Europe in terms of spreading social anarchy surmounted by military despotism. Nietzsche, in so many respects the profoundest of those who united the metaphysical and the esthetic into a sense of tragedy, again and again in his works prophesied inexorable decline. Across the Atlantic, the two Adamses, Brooks and Henry, despaired of Western civilization surviving, based as it was on technology and mass democracy, to both of which, the Adams thought, Western man had in effect transferred his native energies.

The art of the century reveals the malaise I am describing as sensitively as any medium could. Jacques Barzun, in his recent *The Use and Abuse of Art*, takes scholarly note of this. Pointing out how the spirit of destructivenss began in Germany right after Hegel among the so-called *Freien* who flourished in Berlin and whose motto was "Everything that exists is dung," Barzun notes that the revolutionary zeal generated in 1848 for a time swallowed up this cultural nihilism. But it did not die. Barzun writes:

> Its opportunity came when the religion of art had made enough converts to be more than a strict sect; I mean when it was no longer necessary to be a true and qualified devotee of art in order to side with its position. The disenchantment with industrial progress, the distaste for the new democratic tone of life, the technical criticism of mechanistic science—all made recruits for the party of art; so that when the gloom of Realism and Respectability began to seem a nightmare that would never end, the awakening and revolt came about in the name of Art. It was the artists of England, France, and Germany who found the slogans and struck the attitudes by which Victorianism was debunked and destroyed.

Again the truth of the words I quoted early in this book from the late distinguished scientist Eugene Rabinowitch is demonstrated: "The voice of the artist," Rabinowitch writes, "is often the first to respond. . . . Thus, the impending breakdown of the existing order of things, of the generally accepted system of values, should be—and often is—first recognizable in a revolt against the values and canons that had dominated artistic creation; a revolution in art precedes the revolution in society."

Not alone in painting, of course, did the spirit Barzun describes make itself felt in the arts. Throughout the century we can find the thread of disillusion and disenchantment running through literature. In England the novels of Thomas Love Peacock show early distaste in the form of elegant satire of reigning intellectual and moral idols. There were, as we have seen, Blake's prophetic poetry and drawings, expressing an attitude toward emerging capitalism that would only later reach philosophers and sociologists. Wordsworth and Coleridge, in the beginning fascinated by the tides of revolution, increasingly turned their backs on modernity in all its manifestations. Matthew Arnold's *Culture and Anarchy* supplied

themes and insights which would only much later enter into what
was called the sociology of knowledge. There was John Ruskin,
whose celebration of the Pre-Raphaelite painters contained, like the
Pre-Raphaelites' works, a whole implicit philosophy not of progress
but of regress, and with it harsh indictment of industrialism and
mass democracy. Not to be overlooked either is James Thomson's
superbly written dirge, *The City of Dreadful Night*, of which disillusion and despair are the very essence. In lighter but not less serious
vein in England were *The Yellow Book* and the coterie which surrounded it, dedicated to the caricature of Victorian ideals of culture.

Nor was it different in France. Balzac, Stendhal, Flaubert, Zola,
and others, landscapists and portraitists all, left little doubt of what
their view was of the society around them, a view that ranged from
the somber to the hostile. In the early novels of J. K. Huysmans,
Against the Grain and *At the Bottom*, written before his conversion to
Roman Catholicism, the blemishes on the face of progress are
shown as malignancies. Remy de Gourmont wrote in comparable
vein; and Verlaine, Baudelaire, and Mallarmé gave poetic expression to the whole malaise.

This highly visible malaise takes the form, I suggest, of an inversion of the spirit of progress. This spirit, expressed by Browning's
"God's in his Heaven—All's right with the world"; by Herbert
Spencer's "progress is therefore not an accident but a necessity"; by
Marx's confidence, based upon his discovery of "iron laws of motion," in a classless future where man would for the first time
become truly liberated; and by John Stuart Mill's liberalism based
on "one very simple principle," that is, the freedom of the individual from all needless authorities—this whole spirit of progress becomes inverted in those minds I am dealing with in this chapter.
The very conditions or values from which prophets of progress had
derived their panoramic future of hope are shown to be productive
not of progress but of decline, decay, and eventual breakdown. It is
the dark underside of progress that is made manifest by those I
have mentioned here. To quote Jacques Barzun again: "The world

was being turned upside down. The chief men being listened to held their audience by inverting 'truths'—systematic inversion."

We see this disillusion among the sociologists. Scientists they were indeed, at least in objective, concerned overwhelmingly, as we have seen in this book, with accurate renderings of the social landscape and its dominant role-types. But just as the spirit of art obviously entered these renderings, so the artistic malaise I write about here entered into their responses to the science around them. Toennies, Weber, Durkheim, and Simmel all, without exception, can be seen to be ambivalent about the very progress that was being so widely hailed by others as different as Marx and Spencer. Much of the ideological variety we find in contemporary sociology, and, for that matter, the frequent lack of conceptual clarity in treatments of organization and disorganization springs, I would argue, from the ambivalence I have described.

LOSS OF COMMUNITY

When Ferdinand Toennies published *Gemeinschaft und Gesellschaft* in 1887, he gave lasting expression to a contrast that had become more and more evident in the social writing of the nineteenth century, beginning, as I have noted, in the conservative and Romantic movements early in the century. The contrast is, of course, between community, using that word in its largest sense, which is implicit in Toennies's *Gemeinschaft*, and large-scale, secular, individualistic, industrial-national society that seemed to be coming into existence everywhere in the West during the century. *Gesellschaft* is the word Toennies chose for this new society, and although he strove to set it in contexts of moral detachment and objectivity, it is impossible to miss the essentially negative connotation it has in his work of loss of community.

The kind of society that had for Adam Smith, David Ricardo, and other prophets of the industrial system carried the promise of a higher freedom for modern man, carried something quite different for Toennies: not freedom but increasing anonymity, displacement, and deprivation of the sense of organic relatedness to others. From Toennies's point of view, in sum, economic progress carried with it an inversion of human estate, one bound up with the very premises of the new system.

Toennies was in no sense a political reactionary or even conservative. He was a member of liberal movements and voiced strong opposition to the currents of nationalism and anti-Semitism which were to culminate in Nazism. No one acquainted with him, however, thought him other than rather conservative in *temperament*, fundamentally antagonistic to a great many of the elements of political and economic modernity. It is of some interest to know that he was himself an accomplished poet and, before the end of his life (he died in 1936, aged eighty-one), something of a religious believer.

The important point here, however, is the image that Toennies's classic acquired almost from the day of its publication and retained thereafter, of being profoundly negative in its representation of modern society as *Gesellschaft*, which for Toennies meant the whole complex of impersonal, abstract, and anonymous relationships which characterized capitalism, nationalism, and all the forces of individualism, bureaucratization, and secularism which he could see eating away at the social fabric.

Conversely, no reader can remain blind to Toennies's extremely positive treatment of *Gemeinschaft* and of the social structures and forms of human mentality associated with it. In kinship, religion, village, and social class, overwhelmingly in their medieval forms, Toennies found that kind of society which he thought organic and vital and which had been largely destroyed or greatly diminished under the impact of modernity. Marx could see destruction in the fate of village and kinship and religion, but for him such destruction was creative in its long-run implication. For, however intolerable capitalism might be socially and morally to human beings, it was only the prelude to the achievement of a form of human community that would be far more benign than anything represented by the unities of the past—family, village, church, and the like. There is no such optimism, however, in Toennies. No more than

Weber, Durkheim, or Simmel does he see certain, or even probable, community rising from present disorder, impersonality, conflict, and alienation.

Toennies's differentiation of his two great types of society is
deeply rooted in his envisagement of what happened, historically,
to medieval society and the distinctive kinds of motivation and in-
centive, as well as social structure, to be found there. There is a
great deal in common between Toennies's contrast of the medieval
and modern periods and that of Carlyle, say in *Past and Present*,
though there is no evidence I have come across to suggest any
direct influence of Carlyle on Toennies. There didn't have to be.
As we have already seen, explicit or implicit contrast of the Middle
Ages and the modern period was one of the most powerful guiding
themes in art and philosophy alike in the nineteenth century.

It is most assuredly a guiding theme in Toennies's book; though,
writing as a sociologist-philosopher concerned with more than the
narration of European history, he sought to make universal his two
typologies of social order and indeed succeeded, for the *Gemeins-
chaft-Gesellschaft* construct has been widely used by social sciences in
application to the most diverse peoples and cultures.

The essence of Toennies's book can be succinctly stated with respect to what I am here referring to as "the rust of progress." Like
a great many artists and philosophers of his day, he declares that
the achievement of progress, as commonly defined in terms of industry, democracy, technology, individualism, and equality, has
carried with its dislodgments of status, rents in the social fabric,
and transformations of identity which have in turn led to a prolifer-
ation of moral, social, and psychological problems. It could have
been any of a dozen major essayists, poets or novelists (style perhaps excepted!) who wrote the following passage in Toennies's
book:

Gesellschaft deals with the artificial construction of an aggregate of human
beings which superficially resembles *Gemeinschaft* insofar as the individuals
live and dwell together peacefully. However, in *Gemeinschaft* they remain
essentially united in spite of all separating factors, whereas in *Gesellschaft*
they are essentially separated in spite of all uniting factors.

Forty years earlier Disraeli had written in *Sybil:* "There is no community in England; there is aggregation, but aggregation under circumstances which make it rather a dissociating than a unifying principle. . . . Modern society acknowledges no neighbor."

The fundamental reason for the rise in the number of social problems, conflicts, tensions, and torments of one kind or other in modern man's life lies, Toennies tells us, in the gradual erosion of the customs and traditions by which human beings once lived. And this erosion is caused in considerable part by the very nature of the modern political state.

The state frees itself more and more from the traditions and customs of the past and the belief in their importance. . . . The state and its departments and the individuals are the only remaining agents, instead of numerous and manifold fellowships, communities, and commonwealths which grow up organically. The characters of the people, which were influenced and determined by these previously existing institutions, undergo new changes in adaptation to new and arbitrary legal constructions. These earlier institutions lose the firm hold which folkways, mores, and the conviction of their infallibility gave to them.

With only a few alterations, such a passage would have fit easily into Matthey Arnold's *Culture and Anarchy,* and, in meter, into *The City of Dreadful Night,* a poem that has few equals in that age of our own for sheer unrelieved pessimism and melancholy, the consequence of a sensitive mind's reaction to the tides of what so many thought of in the nineteenth century as progress. Nor did Toennies see any imminent solution to the "social problem" that was caused, in his view, by the conflict between a yearning for the values of *Gemeinschaft* and the responses inexorably generated in the public mind by the constitutive qualities of *Gesellschaft.*

A great transformation takes place. Whereas previously the whole of life was nurtured and arose from the profoundness of the people (*Volk*), the capitalistic society through a long process spreads itself over the totality of this people, indeed over the whole of mankind. . . . This process, which does not stop with conferring equal political rights on all citizens, to a certain extent closes the always widening hiatus between the wealth monopoly of the narrow and real *Gesellschaft* and the poverty of the people, but it cannot change the essential character of the hiatus. Indeed, it deepens it, spreading and strengthening the consciousness of the "social question."

There were socialists and others in Toennies's age who could have agreed with the diagnosis, the while preserving confidence in the capacity of organized political will to cure the ailment. There is little, however, to suggest that Toennies was among them, even though, most assuredly, he did not retreat from participation in the social and political order.

ANOMIE

During the nineteenth century the material base of life in Western society rose by an extent not only unprecedented in human history but well beyond anything to be found even in the utopias of earlier centuries. I am referring, of course, to the extraordinary achievements in technology, in mass production of goods, in spread of the foundations of public health, better housing, popular education, and inexpensive recreations, and in longevity. No one, least of all socialists like Karl Marx, disputed the sheer material or technical gains in human life in Western Europe during the century.

Unfortunately, as Durkheim made clear in his sociology, human expectations increased even faster than did life's material improvements. The result was, Durkheim thought, a spirit of pessimism, of moral uncertainty, and dislocation of norms that was out of all harmony with the material progress that was a matter of record. In his *Moral Education* Durkheim writes: "What could be more disillusioning than to proceed toward a terminal point that is nonexistent, since it recedes in the same measure that one advances?" In many areas of philosophy and the arts this question was being asked in Durkheim's day, as indeed it has continued to be asked in our own. Disillusionment was the price human beings were paying for material improvements their ancestors could hardly have dreamed of. So wrote Neitzsche in Germany, the Symbolists in France, and, across the Atlantic, Henry and Brooks Adams, and even Mark Twain, whose hatred of modernity is the dark underside of a great deal that he wrote.

It is disillusionment with precisely those areas of life labeled "progressive," Durkheim continued, that is the chief element of surrounding pessimism. For such areas have had the unforeseen effect of raising, then blasting, man's hopes. "That is why historical periods like ours, which have known the malady of infinite aspiration, are necessarily touched with pessimism. Pessimism always accompanies unlimited aspirations. Goethe's Faust may be regarded as representing par excellence this view of the infinite. And it is not without reason that the poet has portrayed him as laboring in continual anguish."

This is precisely the condition that some of the Romantic writers had foreseen for Western society; for example, in the works of Coleridge, Southey, and Carlyle, perceptions of material progress are accompanied by prophecies of breakdown in the spiritual nature of Western society. The philosopher-theologian Lamennais, while still young and in service to the church he later broke with, wrote in his *Essay on Indifference*, in 1817: "All that has been given man since the Reformation in the way of freedom will become, for lack of supporting faith, mere dust." And in an essay on suicide, written in 1819, which clearly anticipates what Durkheim would write at the end of the century, Lamennais declared: "As man moves away from order, anguish presses around him. He is the king of his own misery, a degraded sovereign in revolt against himself, without duties, without bonds, without society. Alone in the midst of the universe, he runs, or rather he seeks to run, into nothingness." No existentialist of the twentieth century, not Sartre, not Camus, would improve upon that statement.

Tocqueville also foresaw, in the second part of *Democracy in America*, this consequence of modernity, particularly of the circumstances generated by equality. Such circumstances raise man's expectations but at the same time "blast his hopes" for realizing them. Nowhere, Tocqueville went on, does the individual feel more impotent, or so lonely, as he does in the presence of an ascendant public opinion. The literary critic and philosopher Emile Faguet was to make this the basis of his assaults on democracy: the further the mass advances in its power, the more the individual recedes in importance. Much of the poetry that was written in Durkheim's time—by Verlaine and Rimbaud, among others—testifies to the profound sense of the erosion of individuality in the society produced by democracy. The issues, in short, which Durkheim deals with empirically and even quantitatively in his works are very much reflections of issues which had been regnant in French literary and philosophical thought since at least the Restoration.

In his first major book, *Division of Labor* (1893), Durkheim, although primarily concerned to describe the evolutionary progress of society from "mechanical" to "organic" solidarity, takes note of the tendency for the level of advancement of society to be inversely related to human happiness. There is, he tells us, no evident problem of unhappiness in primitive society, no forms of behavior such as suicide to measure the underlying dissatisfaction with life on the part of the individual. By very virtue of the technological and social simplicity of primitive society, there is little if any spur to increase primitive man's desires or his expectations of the future. So great is the solidarity found in primitive and folk society, Durkheim tells us, there can be few if any instances of the kind of anonymity and alienation that besets modern Western man. Modernity has, in sum, brought with it progress, yes, but also a heightening of the individual's sense of isolation, of feeling of insecurity, and, increasingly, of loss of purpose in living. All of this analysis was brought to a focus in Durkheim's study of suicide. In the increase of suicide in the West, Durkheim thought, the malaise of an entire society could be seen and assessed.

We do not diminish Durkheim's stature as social scientist in noting that such analysis, such perspective, had made its appearance early in the century in art and philosophy. Ideas of Faustian aspiration, of defeated expectations and crippling egoism, were rife, as was the theme of suicide, in much of the imaginative literature of the Romantic movement early in the nineteenth century. Durkheim's own admiration for the medieval guild was drawn from currents of renascent medievalism first to be seen among artists. Did he acquire his obsessive interest in religion (though he remained an announced agnostic throughout his life) from the same currents? How interesting that Durkheim's contemporary, the novelist J. K. Huysmans, after dealing with the malignancies of the surrounding society in relentless detail in his early novels, especially *At the Bottom*, where modern man is revealed as shorn of faith or sense or purpose, seeking blindly to destroy himself through excesses in the egoism that is but the other side of loss of moral authority, should turn, following conversion to Roman Catholicism, to a series of novels in which religion is portrayed as bulwark, fortress, above all community.

Durkheim was assuredly no convert. But that is not the essence of the matter. What is the essence is Durkheim's parallel turning, as sociologist to be sure, from early preoccupation with the disorganization of modern society, the malignancy of egoism, and the anomie which he saw as the true index of modernity's inroads into stable structure and belief, to religion. From the time Durkheim completed *Suicide* he seldom if ever deviated, until the outbreak of World War I, from religion as the subject of his researches. Never as a convert, but as a sociologist, he manifests precisely the same kind of interest in religion we find in a Huysmans—and much earlier in the century in Chateaubriand's *Genius of Christianity*—and this interest is, of course, in ritual, cult, the sense of the sacred, and, above all, religion as community, as fortress, as indispensable source of strength for the individual communicant. Agnostic or no, Durkheim succeeded in writing what is beyond doubt the most impressive *scholarly* demonstration of the functional indispensability of religion to society that we have even to this day.

Nor can we set Durkheim's study of religion solely in a scientific context. He was profoundly, almost obsessively, aware of moral crisis in his time. No religious poet or novelist of the time could have set forth more eloquently or determinedly this crisis than does Durkheim. History, he writes in *Moral Education*, reveals "no crisis as serious as that in which European societies have been involved for more than a century. Collective discipline in its traditional form has lost its authority, as the divergent tendencies troubling the public conscience and the resulting general anxiety demonstrate."

It is exceedingly unlikely that Durkheim, who virtually adored science (and we have not even yet produced his superior as a social scientist), would have welcomed any ascription of artistic or esthetic motivation to his work, any more than he would have welcomed religious ascription. Unremitting scientific and scholarly discipline was the law of his life. It is therefore all the more striking, and confirming from my own point of view, that there should be such vivid and profound likeness between the essential themes of Durkheim's work and the themes which are to be found in so much of the art of his time, sacred and secular. Whatever may have been the strictly individual sources of Durkheim's vision of a great moral crisis in his age, of his interest in such manifestations of this crisis as anomie, alienation, repudiation of affluence, and loss of sense of purpose, and, finally, of his distinctive interest in the communal character of religion, its roots in the sacred community, the inescapable fact is that both the vision and the interest are major elements of the art and literature of his day and had been since the early part of the century. No one gives more vivid testimony than Durkheim, in short, to the unity of art and science.

ESTRANGEMENT

Isolation, reserve, alienation, or estrangement: these are for Simmel dominating aspects of the human spirit as the result in very large part of the growth of metropolis, which for Simmel is the very image of modernity. To be sure, Simmel, like Hegel before him, saw some degree of estrangement latent in the very character of the human mind; the character that permits each of us to be, at one and the same time, object as well as subject. But the whole force of modern technological, economic, and political change has been to develop, Simmel thought, a massive objectivism before which the mind of the individual withdraws into itself.

In nearly all respects Simmel is as much the artist as he is the social scientist or philosopher. No one in his day or since vies with

Simmel in either the impressionistic sensitivity with which he regarded the society around him or his grace and subtlety of style. The essay is for Simmel as natural a mode of expression as ever it was for Montaigne, Addison, or Sainte-Beuve. Only Lord Keynes among social scientists of the past hundred years rivals Simmel as artist-essayist. Interestingly, just as Keynes was a member of the famous Bloomsbury group in London, composed largely of writers and painters, so Simmel had almost equally close relation to the group, the "circle," that surrounded the famous esthete Stefan George in Berlin early in the century, one also composed largely of artists and poets. It comes as no surprise to learn that the range of Simmel's esthetic interests was very wide. His courses on the philosophy of art were among the most popular at the University of Berlin, where he was first student, then professor. And not only was he an accomplished essayist-critic of prominent writers and artists of his day, but he is also the author of respectable full-length studies of Goethe and Rembrandt. We learn that he was friend and benefactor of the young Rilke, and his admiration for and study of the French sculptor Rodin is well known on the basis of frequent references. From childhood on, Simmel was deeply interested in all spheres of art.

No artist or esthetician ever gave more attention to that perennial problem of the artist, form or structure, than did Simmel. It was form indeed that became for Simmel the very hallmark of sociology. He lived in an age in the history of the German university when it was considered vital to give precise definition to any field that one sought to introduce into the German university when it was considered vital to give precise definition to any field that one sought to introduce into the German curriculum, and Simmel's contribution was his insistence that it is to *form* that we must look when we are seeking sociology's role among the social scientists. Other disciplines may deal with the content of social relationships: religion, politics, business, recreation, war, education, whatever. Sociology, Simmel argued, must be the discipline in which concern with form or structure transcends interest in content. Thus the dyad or triad may have a political or religious or economic content, and such content is by no means unimportant or irrelevant to the sociologist's inquiry. But the overriding interest of the sociologist will be, Simmel thought, in the structure itself, in the dyadic or triadic relation among individuals, and in the determining or conditioning effect this structure has upon the content.

To discover and identify the forms which the study of human behavior makes possible: this was Simmel's deepest objective as sociologist. What Etienne Gilson, in the work I have several times referred to in this book, *Painting and Reality,* has written on the relation of the artist to forms is instructive in our appreciation of Simmel. "The creative artist, whose imagination is haunted by rudiments of indistinct forms, is a man whose hand will make them really be what they obscurely aspire to become. To enable him to see his own images, the hand of the painter must give them actual being." It is said that Michelangelo once replied to a questioner concerning one of his sculptures by saying that he simply cut and chipped away the large block of marble until he had reached the perfect figure within; then he knew his task was completed.

Simmel too was the seeker of forms: social and psychological as well as esthetic. Just as the mathematician (artist supreme by Simmel's standards) is concerned with the square or triangle as an abstract form, and pursues conclusions regarding this form which are in no way dependent upon what any given square or triangle is actually composed of, so, Simmel tells us, the sociologist studies forms of social interaction more or less in abstraction from the content or objectives the forms embody. Thus in what is widely regarded as his greatest work in sociology, his *Philosophy of Money,* Simmel, working in considerable degree from his early reading of Marx, argues that the significance of money is much wider than what Marx had given it in *Capital.* Not only does money serve as a vital means of exchange in capitalist economy, in contrast to an economy of use or barter; it is, in its several manifestations, of metal, paper, credit, and faith, a form of social interaction that is closely associated with other forms, mental, social, and cultural, in

modern society. For Simmel the appearance and quick spread of
money in the late Middle Ages was but a single example of a far
greater phenomenon in modern history: "the rational world-
outlook" through which organic unities became dissolved into mere
classes or orders of social relationship with the individual achieving
a degree of liberation, and in time separateness, even isolation, that
was impossible in such a society as that which had reached its
height in the thirteenth century. Money thus becomes for Simmel
not only the "content," so to speak, of a new form of economic system; it is by its nature a form of human interaction and com-
munication, one that permits the conversion of qualitative values to
quantitative ones but also the release of individual elements from
communal contexts, thus allowing the endless formation of new
and ever-changing relationships.

Simmel's preoccupation with form was part and parcel of what
was perhaps the single most momentous change taking place in the
worlds of art and science alike at the beginning of the twentieth
century. What had been conceived of as "matter"—hard, unchang-
ing, solid, and irreducible by definition—in the mechanics of the
nineteenth century, and differentiated so sharply from energy or
motion, now became, in the works of the great pioneering physi-
cists of our own age, the mere manifestion of pure energy revealing
itself in relations expressible only in mathematical terms. Increasingly for the scientist, reality could be understood only in terms of
elemental patterns or figures—as indeed that greatest of philos-
opher-mathematicians, Plato, had declared more than two thousand years earlier.

But very much the same change was taking place in the world of
painting, and also, though in less striking degree, in literature.
Here too we observe a novel concentration upon structures and
patterns, and also upon uses of light and shadow, that suggests an
interest in form for its own sake, a conviction that reality lies less in
content than in form. For the artist as for the mathematical physicist, truth or reality was found in the diverse shapes which provided the true foundations of the world and of life. Impressionism

and Symbolism were both very much parts of the transformation I am speaking of. The same dissolution of matter or content in the traditional representation of reality took place, with emphasis transferred from literal imitation or copy by the craftsman to the use of symbols and allusions from which the viewer would make his way intuitively to what lay within the shapes of these symbols and allusions. What Jacques Barzun writes is instructive here:

> There is no evidence that the artists who took the path away from nature to symbol were tempted by curiosity about the work of Bohr and Planck or by envy of the Nobel Prize in Physics. A pervasive sophistication (as it was called) was at work. . . . We see it first in the theory of art that ushers in the twentieth century, the theory of art as pure form, relations only.

Simmel's place in this "pervasive sophistication" is a clear one, made manifest in a host of works pertaining to art and metaphysics as well as to sociology. The pursuit of knowledge became for him essentially a single, albeit broad, avenue: one leading to the realization of shapes and forms, with matter or content left indistinct and relatively unimportant. I have referred briefly to Simmel's fascination with dyads and triads in human relationships irrespective of their content or "matter." The same fascination extended to small groups generally, and to the basic processes which were contained in them so far as the larger social order was concerned. Such small groups were for Simmel the molecules of the social order, and his interest in them was almost exclusively that of the mathematician-artist—an interest in shape rather than in what was embodied in the way of norm or objective. Thus in Simmel's matchless studies of friendship, dependence, gratitude, love, and confidence, to name but a few such relations, he gives us insight into forms in much the fashion of the artist. Like the artist, Simmel constantly searches for the elemental, and he never disdains the uses of intuition, of what we call creative inspiration. To read Simmel on the distinction between friendship and love, on the difficulty, nay impossibility, of sexual love becoming genuinely united with friendship in the classic sense of the latter, is to read passages of intuitive insight which are equaled only in the writings of the better poets and novelists. Here, too, it is interesting to realize, there is affinity between Simmel's deepest currents of thought and those in the world of literature. For just as a major transformation of painting and sculpture was taking place at the beginning of the present century, so was one taking place in literature. Waning now, for the most part, was the kind of objective, "out there" world that had been depicted by a Dickens, a Balzac, or a Tolstoy. In its place was emerging the very different world conceived by such diverse writers as Proust, Joyce, Virginia Woolf, and so many others in the early twentieth century, a world much more subjective, much more an emanation of the writer's ego in relation to a perceived world, a product of what was increasingly being regarded as the writer's stream of consciousness. To this world Simmel, above any of the major sociologists of his day, belonged in spirit. If he avoided the profound egocentricity of a Max Stirner and the phenomenology of a Husserl, at least in degree, Simmel yet manifests elements of these currents of thought in a measure not found in Toennies and Durkheim and only in relatively slight adumbrations by Weber.

Simmel reveals the same inverted view of progress we find in the others I have dealt with in this chapter. One does not find the implicit pessimism in Simmel that is so apparent in Weber and, in less extent, in Durkheim and Toennies. But his basic view of the toll exacted by the political and economic advance of modernity is scarcely different. In his *Sociology of Religion* he writes:

I see the most capacious and far-reaching collision between society and the individual, not in the aspect of particular interests but in the general form of individual life. Society aspires to totality and organic unity, each of its members constituting but a component part. The individual as part of the society has to fulfill special functions and employ all his strength; he is expected to modify his skills so that he will become the best-qualified performer of these functions. But this role is opposed by man's bent toward unity and totality as an expression of his own individuality.

Simmel had no doubt of his epoch's general decadence, the advancing deterioration of the values by which the West had lived for so long. He was, so far as we can determine, one with Stefan

George and other members of "the circle" in Berlin in this respect. There is not in Simmel the same explicit yearning for the advent of leaders of heroic stature who might save Germany and the West from the leveled mediocrity, the homogeneous conformity, and the dearth of genuine creative talent in culture and politics that we find in the utterances of George and others in his group. But there is without doubt the same perception of the nature of the problem presented by mass society and the tides of democratic industrialism.

In his beautiful essay "The Ruin," Simmel uses the ruin of a monument or temple as the symbol of the progressive ruin of moral codes and social structures. In any physical ruin, Simmel writes, we see

purpose and accident, nature and spirit, past and present, resolve the tension of their contrasts. It is as though a segment of existence must collapse before it can become unresistant to all currents and powers coming from all corners of reality. Perhaps this is the reason for our general fascination with decay and decadence, a fascination which goes beyond what is merely negative and degrading. The rich and many-sided culture, the unlimited *impressionability*, and the understanding open to everything, which are characteristic of decadent epochs, do signify this coming together of all contradictory strivings. An equalizing justice connects the uninhibited unity of all things that grow apart and against one another with the decay of those men and the works of men which now can only yield but can no longer create and maintain their own forms out of their own strength.

As decadence is one of the identifying attributes of the modern era, so is the widening sense of individual isolation, of estrangement from fellows, from integrating values, even from self. In another of his essays, "The Stranger," Simmel, with characteristic skill in uniting past and present, the symbolic and real, takes the stranger as a role-type, as a social form throughout history, for his subject, defining the stranger in terms of his "liberation" from every point in space and also in time. For Simmel the stranger possesses striking symbolic value for the modern West. The stranger is "the person who comes today and stays tomorrow." It is this fixity of role-position that gives identity to the modern "wanderer" through space and time, rootless, detached, and permanently estranged from all that is stationary in hope and expectation.

Of all manifestations of the rust of progress, the largest for Simmel is precisely this isolation, alienation, of the individual. Again and again we find references to it in his writings. Thus in his classic study of the secret society—the single work, I think, that most epitomizes the diversity of Simmel's genius—we find, along with treatment of the form itself, insights into the special kind of "secrecy" that comes in modern Western society from the individual's loss of the true intimacy, friendship, and love his forebears knew. The loss of the organic society, with its concentric circles of membership, which had reached its high point in the Middle Ages (on this point Simmel is one with Toennies), has resulted in an impersonality of the social order that carries with it anonymity and enforced reserve for the individual. The burden that is placed upon friendship and love alike by the increasing inability of the individual to give of himself as freely to others as had once been the case is, Simmel writes, a heavy one for modern man. The individual in our time, Simmel continues, "has too much to hide" to make possible the closeness of relationships, especially the relationship of friends, that was once a virtual commonplace when social ties were overwhelmingly personal in character.

It is not only the sense of community that has suffered. Man himself has become diminished by the weight of the "objectivity" of modern culture. "If, for instance, we view the immense culture which for the last hundred years has been embodied in things and in knowledge, in institutions and in comforts, and if we compare all this with the cultural progress of the individual during the same period—at least in high status groups—a frightful disproportion in growth between the two becomes evident. Indeed, at some points we notice a retrogression in the culture of the individual with reference to spirituality, delicacy, and idealism."

That view is the basic theme of Simmel's essay "Metropolis and Mental Life," perhaps the best known of all his works. As technology, far-flung industry, and the increasingly bureaucratized state make of society a more and more "objective" thing, so does the individual tend to retreat correspondingly into more frequent states of "subjective" consciousness. "The individual has become a mere cog in an enormous organization of things and powers which tear from his hands all progress, spirituality and value in order to transform them from their subjective form into the form of a purely objective life. It needs merely to be pointed out that metropolis is the genuine arena of this culture which outgrows all personal life." The consequence of this "objectification" of what lies outside the individual is a spreading sense of reserve among individuals, a progressive insulation, as it were, from "the intensification of nervous stimulation" that goes with metropolis and its incessant psychic invasions of the human being.

There is not much difference between metropolis, as Simmel presents it in his essay, and what, a few years after, T. S. Eliot would refer to in *The Wasteland* as "Unreal City." Nor is there substantial difference between the inhabitants of Simmel's metropolis and those whom Eliot called "the hollow men," "the stuffed men." Early in the nineteenth century Carlyle had written: "Not the external and physical alone is now managed by machinery, but the internal and the spiritual also. . . . Men are grown mechanical in head and in heart as well as in hand. . . . Their whole efforts, attachments, opinions, turn on mechanism and are of a mechanical nature."

DEGENERATION

One final attribute of the malaise I have been writing of is degeneration: the running-down of things, the replacement of processes of genesis and development by those of decay and decline. Weber, in the final pages of *The Protestant Ethic and the Spirit of Capitalism*, having demonstrated the profound effect of the *spirit*, Protestant and other, behind the material trappings of capitalism, takes note of the demise into which this selfsame spirit has fallen in his own time. No essayist or poet could have inscribed more memorably the essence of this vision of defeat than did Weber: "Today the spirit of religious asceticism—whether finally, who knows?—has escaped from the cage. But victorious capitalism, since it rests on mechanical foundations, needs its support no longer. The rosy blush of its laughing heir, the Enlightenment, seems also to be irretrievably fading, and the idea of duty in one's calling prowls about in our lives like the ghost of dead religious beliefs." Powerful though capitalism might seem when Weber wrote these lines, it was already losing, in short, the popular faith Weber knew to be vital to any institution or set of institutions. Many years later, Weber's fellow-German, Joseph Schumpeter, who became one of America's greatest economists, would make what is essentially Weberian analysis the foundation of his own classic prediction of the eventual downfall of capitalism in *Capitalism, Socialism and Democracy,* one of the most original and profound books of the age.

It was still another German, Max Nordau, a contemporary of Weber, who wrote a long novel, published in 1892–93, titled *Degeneration,* in which he sought to demonstrate that there is a fixed and ineradicable relation between genius and degeneracy: between the existence of a spreading class of intellectuals, along with its achievements, and the moribundity of the social order that contains this class. Well before World War I had commenced in 1914, the German sociologist-historian Oswald Spengler, in his *Decline of the West,* tried, with large if controversial impact, to show that every civilization is, on the record of the past, destined to decline when a certain point of achievement has been reached. The West, declared Spengler, is no exception. The stigmata of decline that Spengler points out for us in Western society are one with those we have already noted in the art, philosophy, and sociology of the end of the century. And, as I have observed, Simmel's moving essay on the special place *ruins* have in modern Western consciousness is testimony to his own perceptive, if never morbid, awareness of the phenomenon of decline and breakdown. Thomas Mann's novels *Buddenbrooks* and especially *The Magic Mountain,* along with a host of shorter works, give us premonitions and prophecies as well as observations of the same ongoing decline and decay.

The state of mind I describe was in no respect confined to Germany. Durkheim took note of it in the final pages of *Suicide* and also in his posthumous *Moral Education*. Even in his earliest work, *The Division of Labor*, although it would be inaccurate to speak of any intrinsic pessimism in Durkheim, there is, nonetheless, a great deal of stress upon what he called the decline of consensus, of the moral conscience in society. And in the later works he is emphatic in his insistence that Western society was undergoing a great "moral crisis" of which breakdown might easily be a consequence. The *fin de siècle* spirit in France needs no further description here: it suffices to say that writers such as Remy de Gourmont, Huysmans, Peguy, Proust, and Verlaine took very much the same view of the world around them and retreated from it accordingly, albeit in diverse ways.

Even in the United States at the turn of the century, where the idea of progress undoubtedly had a more compelling importance among intellectuals generally than it did in Europe at the time, we do not lack for prophets of breakdown. Among them are Henry and Brooks Adams. The former, in his *Degradation of the Democratic Dogma*, in numerous letters and occasional pieces, and in both *Mont St. Michel and Chartres* and the famous *Education*, made vivid his sense of despair so far as American democracy, indeed Western society, were concerned. He divided the past into the ages of instinct, religion, science, and then the "supersensual." Each age is shorter than its predecessor, with the final age the shortest by far. Throughout the evolutionary process, Henry Adams thought, there has been a constant depletion of human energy. The next hundred years, he wrote, would see an "ultimate colossal, cosmic collapse." Henry's brother Brooks put the matter somewhat differently but with an analogous point. There is, Brooks Adams wrote, a "law of civilization and decay." It is cyclical in nature. There are recurring periods in mankind's history of rise. But so are there, inexorably, periods of decay and breakdown. Such a period, Brooks Adams, believes, is our own.

It cannot be said that many American sociologists during the first half of the twentieth century spent much time speculating on

large-scale processes of decline in civilization, though the idea
hovers nevertheless over the scene, manifest in some of the writings
of Sumner, for example, who was far from the optimist he has
sometimes been portrayed as. There were others. But where the
spirit or psychology of degeneration is most plainly to be seen in
American sociology, at the very least from the time Charles H.
Cooley wrote, is in the almost obsessive regard we find for the
whole idea of *social disorganization*, a concept that by the early part
of the twentieth century had come increasingly to supplant the
older term "social problems." The idea that the assertedly pathological forms of behavior to be found in society—crime, poverty,
divorce, alcoholism, mental illness, etc.—were more than the dis-
crete violations of ordinary morality they had for so long been held
to be and were instead symptoms of a process, disorganization,
found throughout society: *this* was in many ways a major change,
perhaps *the* major change, in the nature of sociology in the United
States at the beginning of the century. I believe it is fair to say that
the theme of disorganization, increasingly rivaled at the present
moment by the related theme of deviance, is the one, however
termed and defined, that has hovered over more sociological research and writing than any other in this country. As I say, it
would be inaccurate, looking back on the writings of American
sociologists over the past three-quarters of a century, to ascribe to
them any great philosophical principle of degeneration or breakdown, comparable to what may be found in so much European
writing during the same period. The American sociological mind
has not often been given to philosophy of history, to what has
recently come to be called macrosociology, although recent indica-
tions suggest this condition may be changing substantially at the
present time.

But in whatever form, however worked into the structure of
sociological thought, the theme of degeneration has been a signal
one from the time when Comte—believing profoundly in what he
called "the spiritual crisis of our age," caused by the radical depredations upon tradition and stability of the two revolutions and

quickened by the individualism that Comte pronounced "the disease of the Western world"—brought into being for the first time the word *sociology*.

Not only Comte but the long succession of sociologists who have proved to exert the greatest effect upon the contemporary sociological mind would find the famous lines from Yeats perfectly appropriate to, indeed constitutive of, Comte's science:

> Things fall apart; the center cannot hold; . . .
> The blood-dimmed tide is loosed, and everywhere
> The ceremony of innocence is drowned;
> The best lack all conviction, while the worst
> Are full of passionate intensity.

Index